SNAPDRAGON

SNAPDRAGON

The Story of John Henry Newman

By JOYCE SUGG

with illustrations by
HUGH MARSHALL

*"There used to be much snapdragon growing on the walls
opposite my freshman's rooms there [Trinity College] and
I had for years taken it as the emblem of my own perpetual
residence, unto death, in my University."*

J.H.N. — *Apologia Pro Vita Sua*

Our Sunday Visitor, Inc.
HUNTINGTON

Published by arrangement with C. Goodliffe Neale, Ltd.,
Alcester, England

First U.S. edition published in 1982 by
Our Sunday Visitor, Inc.
200 Noll Plaza
Huntington, Indiana 46750

Text copyright © 1964 by Joyce Sugg.
Illustrations copyright © 1978 by C. Goodliffe Neale, Ltd.

ISBN 0-87973-653-4   LC 81-85242

Nihil obstat: Andreas J. Moore, LCC, Censor deputatus
Imprimatur: Patritius Casey, Vicarius generalis
Westminster, October 9, 1964

PRINTED IN THE UNITED STATES OF AMERICA

Snapdragon

A Riddle for a Flower Book

I am rooted in the wall
Of buttress'd tower or ancient hall;
Prison'd in an art-wrought bed,
Cased in mortar, cramp'd with lead;
Of a living stock alone
Brother of the lifeless stone.

Else unpriz'd, I have my worth
On the spot that gives me birth;
Nature's vast and varied field
Braver flowers than me will yield,
Bold in form and rich in hue,
Children of a purer dew,
Smiling lips and winning eyes
Meet for earthly paradise.
Choice are such,—and yet thou knowest
Highest he whose lot is lowest.
They, proud hearts, a home reject
Framed by human architect.
Humble I can bear to dwell
Near the pale recluse's cell,
And I spread my crimson bloom
Mingled with the cloister's gloom.

Life's gay gifts and honours rare,
Flowers of favour! win and wear!
Rose of beauty, be the queen
In pleasure's ring and festive scene.
Ivy, climb and cluster, where
Lordly oaks vouchsafe a stair.

Vaunt, fair Lily, stately dame,
Pride of birth and pomp of name.
Miser Crocus, starved with cold,
Hide in earth thy timid gold.
Travell'd Dahlia, freely boast
Knowledge brought from foreign coast.
Pleasure, wealth, birth, knowledge, power,
These have each an emblem flower;
So for me alone remains
Lowly thought and cheerful pains.
Be it mine to set restraint
On roving wish and selfish plaint;
And for man's drear haunts to leave
Dewy morn and balmy eve.
Be it mine the barren stone
To deck with green life not its own,
So to soften and to grace
Of human works the rugged face.
Mine, the unseen to display
In the crowded public way,
Where life's busy arts combine
To shut out the Hand Divine.

Ah! no more a scentless flower,
By approving Heaven's high power,
Suddenly my leaves exhale
Fragrance of the Syrian gale.
Ah! 'tis timely comfort given
By the answering breath of Heaven!
May it be! Then well might I
In College cloister live and die.

J.H.N.   October 2nd 1827

Contents

Illustrations

Author's Note

The letter on page 149 is in the possession of the Oratory
School and has appeared in their school magazine, No. 120
(1962). It is reproduced here by kind permission of the
Editor.

   I am very grateful to Miss Meriol Trevor, who not only
helped me to the treasures of information that she had in
store for her large-scale and important biography of Newman, but also encouraged me in the most kind way as I
wrote this book. I should also like to thank my own pupils
of Rye St Antony School, Oxford. A story-teller needs an
audience—and they have been appreciative listeners. I
think that as I tried to help them to know and love Newman, I found him all over again for myself.

                                                      J. S.

1 — *Home and School*

It is the year 1806 and a fine, early morning. Imagine a square, comfortable-looking Georgian house set in lovely gardens by the river, at Ham near Richmond, west of London. The gardener is cutting the lawn, so early in the day, but the family inside is not astir yet. The dew is heavy on the grass and the air is cold, but it will be sunny and warm later on. Upstairs a very small boy called John Henry Newman is lying in his crib wide awake, listening to the ring of the scythe; what a delightful noise it is, a good prelude to another happy day. It would not do, of course, to get up and rush about naughtily before he is called; he is five, and Mama tells him he is a big boy now and must behave accordingly. He is quite content, though, to lie here quietly with his own thoughts. He remembers lying here in his bed at night (it was last November) and instead of the unfriendly dark there was a small, triumphant light from the candles set in the windows to mark the battle of Trafalgar, when the ogre Boney was kept by brave Nelson from coming and pouncing upon good English people in their homes.

It is less exciting, but pleasant, to lie here at the beginning of an ordinary day, wondering what he will do in it. Soon he will go downstairs and see through an open door the breakfast cups set out, very shining and clear. He has an uncommon memory, this small John Henry, and, years and years later, he will be able to turn the pages back and see scene after scene in the life of the small child that he was, every one a clear, bright picture, every one a remembrance of happiness.

We can see him pretty clearly ourselves, standing there in the bright, soft light of morning, at the foot of the stair-

9

case. He is wearing the attractive but impractical clothes that little boys did wear then, trousers in a light buff coloured fabric called nankeen, buttoned high onto a soft, fine shirt, with a carefully laundered frill round his neck. He has blue eyes and unusually strongly marked features for such a young child, with a large nose and mouth and a firm chin. He has brown, soft hair falling straight down over his forehead with no hint of a parting; most little boys have such soft, floppy hair, but John's hair will never settle down to a stiffer tidiness.

What will he do later in the day? There may be a task to do for Papa, reading or arithmetic. He can read perfectly already, and likes to do sums, and Papa, a bluff, hearty man, very kind, and proud of his eldest son, does not scold, but only says when the little boy flags that he will not still be thought a clever boy if he does not go on to learn more. When he is older he is to learn music, and when he is just a little bigger Papa will teach him to play billiards in their rather shabby billiards room. To-day he will perhaps learn some verses of a poem and then he can recite to entertain guests who come to the house. (He began his recitations on his fourth birthday when he said "The Cat and the Cream-Bowl" for a party of little ones.)

Then he will go and play with his younger brother, Charles. He may play Ancient Greeks down by the river; there is an island that is Ithaca and he is Ulysses. And he will go and pick some flowers in the fields and make a rather squashed and short-stalked posy for Mama. Or he will wander in the large kitchen garden and see what is to be had for the picking. (It is so easy to get among the gooseberries of an idle morning, and so hard to get out again!) He will climb into the swing that hangs from the large plane-tree and swing until he is dizzy, right up towards the patch of sky that shines through the green leaves.

There are splendid trees on the lawn, acacias with rough barks, as high as the plane-tree, a Spanish chestnut, a larch.

"Playing with his younger brother Charles"

A large magnolia flowers up the side of the house. The scent of new-cut grass lingers on the air.

It is like the Garden of Paradise here, it is an enchanted ground. Really, that just describes it, for sometimes, when John walks in the garden, or lies and thinks and listens to the sweet sound of the mower's scythe, in his crib in the front room at the top of the house, he has the oddest feeling that this beautiful world might suddenly vanish away, an enchantment, a dream, here and then gone. . . .

The very next year the family moved from Ham, from the never-to-be-forgotten house and from the magic garden. They returned to London, where John Henry had been born on the 21st of February, 1801, and they settled into another comfortable, solid Georgian house, Number 17 Southampton Place. Changes might come for the Newman children but nothing, in their early childhood, shook their security. There was money enough for comfort, provided from their father's banking business. There was discipline at home but not too much. They had a father who was always anxious to do his best for them; they had a mother who was kind and gay. Her ancestors had been French Protestants, Huguenots (her maiden name was a rather strange one, Jemima Fourdrinier) and she had a little touch of French vivacity. She was a sincerely religious woman too, with something of her French forebears' Protestant earnestness, and she taught her children to love the word of God. John Henry would stand at her knee and hear the stories, gaze at the pictures and make out some of the words for himself on the open page of the large Bible.

When he was seven he was sent to school, to Dr Nicholas' school at Ealing, on the west side of London. Papa had heard good things of this school—it was "run on Eton lines" and it "got the boys on".

His parents soon came to see John, and he was desolate when they left him. Dr Nicholas found him crying by himself. He could not stop crying and he could not face the Common Room where the big, tough boys would laugh at his tears. The Headmaster was all hearty reassurance. No, of course they would not say dreadful things! "O Sir, but they will," said John: "They will say all sorts of things. Come and see for yourself!" And he took Dr Nicholas by the hand and led him into the room so that he could hear the taunts. Poor, innocent seven-year-old, he was really surprised to find the other boys quiet and respectful the moment the Headmaster was inside the door.

It was a rough hurly-burly for a small, shy boy straight from home, but it might have been much worse. The Headmaster of Eton at that time was flogging boys by dozens every day, and at Rugby the big boys were roasting fags and tossing them in blankets.

John settled down to master Latin and Greek. He was promoted from class to class with great speed; Dr Nicholas said he had never had a boy who went up the school so fast. The other boys liked him, even if he did race them up the school, for he was a person of great charm, not an insipid boy, but one who was full of good ideas. He wrote a magazine called "The Spy", and then, since he liked being busy and hated to get into a rut, he started another paper called "The Anti-Spy". There was the Spy Club, too, of which he was Founder and Grand Master. The Members met and wore special ribbons and made speeches. One of the boys drew a picture of the Grand Master haranguing the Club; it is not a good picture, but you can recognise John Henry by his large nose.

There were other diversions too, such as collecting riddles. Here are some that he wrote down to try out on somebody:

Which has most legs, a horse or no horse?
No horse has five legs.

Which is the greatest Friday in the year?
Shrove Tuesday.

What colour are the winds and storms?
Storms arose and winds blew.

He made kites and flew them. (He made one specially fine one, with glass eyes for its face.) And he learned to play the violin and loved to make music and hear it. Sometimes when there was music in the drawing-room, Dr Nicholas would let John and other musical boys come in to listen.

Dr Nicholas was a very kind man. Once he stopped young Newman as he was scurrying on his way and said, "Why, John, it's your birthday—won't they be drinking your health at home to-day? I must go to London to-day—suppose you get up behind the carriage and then you can say I shall be glad of a dinner too."

John quite appreciated the proposal. He hopped up with the greatest alacrity. To dine with Mama and Papa and to have their loving birthday wishes, and to see his sisters running down from the nursery, twittering with excitement like little birds to see John unexpectedly, and on his birthday too—and to eat his favourite dishes at the family table instead of having the usual school victuals! This really was a treat.

One of John's great pleasures was to act in the annual Latin play at school. He even made some verses on this topic:

> Sweet is the notice that proclaims that all
> May lie in bed until a later call;
> Sweet is December first, or first of June
> That shows the holidays are coming soon;
> Sweet is the hour that hails the incipient rule
> Of the new captain of our numerous school.
> But far more dear the glad, auspicious day
> The Doctor tells us we may have a play.

But really the best part of school was the looking forward to the holidays. Dr Nicholas required the boys to send home notice of the end of term, and to do it in their best writing, and so John wrote carefully:

14

Dear Mama,

I have again the pleasure to announce the approach of our vacation. It begins as usual on the 21st instant, when I hope to see you as well as it leaves,

dear Mama,

Your dutiful son,

JOHN HENRY NEWMAN.

In his private Journal, though, he was more brief and more excited. Sometimes he wrote in cheerful, bad Latin: "Sum ire domum in minore tempore quam hebdomada.* Huzza!" He had a stick towards the end of term and gleefully cut a notch as each day went by.

In the holidays he had a wonderful time with his brothers and sisters. There were six young Newmans altogether—John Henry, Charles, Harriett, Francis, Jemima and Mary. In the summer they were mostly at Norwood with Grandmama and Aunt Betsey, living in Vine Cottage, a delightful, tiny, cosy house, surrounded by fields and woods, which were the haunt of gypsies. The children went bathing and haymaking and rambled about. John enjoyed his hours of solitude too, devouring Scott's novels in bed in the early mornings.

In the winter they were in London, and in the lamplit evenings the family enjoyed music altogether, John playing them Mozart and Scarlatti on his violin. Often they produced plays, and once, an opera. (John wrote the words and music.) He was a good eldest brother, kind to the little ones and thoughtful for Mama. At times he was a little bossy and pompous, as eldest brothers tend to be, and, as far as home plays went, he was probably a kind of Bottom, writing, producing and taking the big parts. He never had it all his own way, however, eldest brother though he was, for all the young Newmans were clever and full of their own ideas, and they would not let themselves be organised too much by anyone. They were all as bright as buttons,

* It means "I am to go home in less than a week."

and holidays, when they were all together, busy with their schemes, were lively times.

Then, dismal day, the beginning of term. The girls sighed and settled down to work at home, and the boys went back to Ealing. Charles was the one who would mind the most; he had his share of Newman brains, but he never settled to work, and even Dr Nicholas could not get him on. Frank, handsome and clever, was happy enough, and John, as we know, was the pride of the place.

No doubt his parents and teachers wondered sometimes what this unusually intelligent and charming boy would be when he grew up. Mr Newman rather hoped he would be a lawyer. Perhaps he would go into Parliament? He was good at making speeches. It would have been a reasonable guess that he would be a writer, for he was always scribbling busily. A person who knew him very well might suppose he would become a poet, not because he tossed off verses about the Latin play, but because of the strange deep workings of his imagination. Later he said of himself as a schoolboy:

> I used to wish the Arabian Tales were true; my imagination ran on unknown influences, on magical powers and talismans . . . I thought life might be a dream, or I an angel, and all this world a deception, my fellow angels by a playful device concealing themselves from me, and deceiving me with the semblance of a material world.

Supposing the magic spells which he liked to think of really existed, and supposing that by means of a spell he could look into the future—what would he think? He would, in fact, become a scholar, a writer, a preacher—and all this he might see with no great surprise. But that he would end as a Cardinal of the Roman Catholic Church! Nothing for it but to disbelieve the magic, for that was the most unlikely thing in the world.

He had picked up the Catholic practice of crossing himself (he was very superstitious and used to do it before going into the dark) but he never knew where he had learned to do this. And he decorated the front of his Latin verse book with a cross and a rosary. He probably copied this from a picture in one of those romantic, gruesome novels of Mrs Radcliffe, that have ghosts of medieval monks in them; but think of his surprise when, thirty years later, Newman turned out his old schoolbook adorned with Catholic symbols.

The truth was that in the years when John Henry Newman was a boy, Catholics and Catholic ideas were little thought of in England. If they were thought of, they were disliked and distrusted, but generally they did not need to be considered. Catholics, driven to it by long years of persecution, were very quiet people, keeping themselves to themselves. This is Newman's own picture of how Catholics looked to him when he was a boy :

Here a set of poor Irishmen, coming and going at harvest-time, or a colony of them lodged in a miserable quarter of the vast metropolis. There, perhaps, an elderly person, seen walking in the streets, grave and solitary, and strange, though noble in bearing, and said to be of good family, and a "Roman Catholic". An old-fashioned house of gloomy appearance, closed in with high walls and an iron gate and yews, and the report attaching to it that "Roman Catholics" lived there; but who they were, or what they did, or what was meant by calling them "Roman Catholics" no-one could tell, though it had an unpleasant sound, and told of form and superstition. And then, perhaps as we went to and fro, looking with a boy's curious eyes through the great city, we might come some day upon some Moravian chapel, or Quaker's meeting house, and to-morrow upon a chapel of the "Roman Catholics"; but nothing was to be gathered from it except that there were lights burning there, and some boys in white, swinging censers; and what it all meant could only be learned from books, from Protestant Histories and Sermons; and they did not report well of the "Roman Catholics" but, on the contrary, deposed that they had once had power and abused it.

So he certainly never considered becoming a Catholic. He probably considered becoming a clergyman in the Church of England, where there would be a good advancement for a clever boy, a place in an Oxford or Cambridge College, perhaps, a comfortable living, and then, perhaps, a Bishopric. He thought of it in those terms, rather than as service for God.

John Henry, aged fourteen or so, was not very religious. When he was a little boy, he was truly religious, not priggishly so, but naturally and happily. He knew, without putting it into words, that it was God who lent the brightness and glory to the early days in his happy garden, and he trusted in God who was watching over him as readily as he trusted his mother and father. Now, as a clever schoolboy, he had grown a hard skin. He liked to read irreligious books sometimes, and to argue with the more godly of the schoolmasters. Oh yes, he agreed that one must try to be virtuous, but why be religious? And what did "loving God" mean? One thing he still cherished— he loved to read the Bible.

Then, when he was fifteen and a half, there came a turning point in his life. That year, 1816, was a most worrying one for Mr and Mrs Newman. Mr Newman was a banker, and his business failed. After much struggle and worry he managed to pay off his creditors. He gave up banking and turned to brewing, and he eventually moved the family from Norwood to Alton. This was a real break from all the young Newmans had loved and known. Norwood was near their native London though in those days it was a country place surrounded by woods and heath land. Alton was down in Hampshire. Mrs Newman was in a great turmoil, and while she tried to console her husband and sort out their domestic affairs, the children ("the dear, dear creatures" as she said in a letter) had to be arranged for. John was left at school all the holidays, although he was due to leave. There he was, ill, worried about his parents, without regular work, and all his friends gone. It was a time for reflection, and he began to take notice of one of the masters, the Reverend Mr Mayers. Mr Mayers was a clergyman of the "Evangelical" kind. The Evangelicals, or "Low Church" people were sternly, strongly Protestant, a sort of latter-day Puritans, having much in common with the Methodists. They had strict notions about the wickedness of dancing and card-playing and such, and tended to use Biblical phrases in their speech. At their worst they were oily and sanctimonious, but at their best (and Mr Mayers was an excellent man) they made the ordinary church-goer seem worldly and superficial, for they believed genuinely and devoutly in the saving power of Jesus Christ. John listened to Mr Mayers now, and read the hard books that he lent him. He saw and repented of his own pride, and he returned to God. All Evangelicals set great store by the moment of "conversion", that time when, under the impulse of a violent emotion, the Christian knew himself to be "saved". John was not sure that his conversion was of the accepted kind; he did not feel a violent change, but rather as if he had returned, by God's grace, to a state of acknowledging and loving Our Lord, which he had known before. But that God had done great things to his soul he was sure, as sure as he was of having hands and feet.

Now he understood his own feeling that the world was a kind of lovely passing show. You could indeed give no final allegiance to this interesting world. In his own famous phrase, he rested, "in the thought of two, and two only, supreme and luminously self-evident beings, myself and my Creator".

So that eventful year, partly sad and partly glorious, drew on to December, and another decisive step was to be taken. John was to go to one of the Universities, but which was it to be? Mr Newman still did not know whether to make for Oxford or Cambridge, though the post-chaise was at the door, and the horses were stamping their hooves. A friend called and advised Oxford. Very well, then! Mr Newman and John climbed up. John could hardly contain his excitement. "To Oxford", cried Papa —and they were off.

2 – Oxford

It was a long drive from London to Oxford in those days, and the December cold was biting John's fingers and toes by the time they came within sight of the city from the high ground just outside. But when he first saw Oxford, cold was dispelled by a warm glow of excitement. It is still a lovely sight to see the city's spires and towers outlined on a pearly winter sky, but in 1816 the city of Oxford was far smaller and more beautiful than it is now. It had no suburbs and no Cowley factories; its streets were quiet and its colleges lay undisturbed and serene, bounded by the river and the willow trees and the surrounding fields and groves.

John Henry Newman loved Oxford from that first moment. He had a mind and heart alive to beauty, ready to love Oxford when he saw her "whispering from her towers the last enchantments of the Middle Ages". He was ready, indeed, to love Oxford not only for her beauty but for the spirit and traditions he would find enshrined there. The first Oxford colleges were built in medieval times so that men could pursue learning and holiness within those halls and cloisters, and still the city's quiet buildings spoke of that twofold quest. Life there was to be a seeking for light—the light of truth, the light of God. *Dominus illuminatio mea*—"The Lord is my Light". The motto of the University spoke straight to his heart. He had solemn thoughts as the post-chaise clattered into the city streets. He came, he felt, as if to a shrine.

Mr Newman stopped first at Exeter College, but there was no place vacant so they went across the Turl to Broad Street as they were directed, to Trinity College. John Henry Newman's name was entered there and back they went to London. They called on Dr Nicholas to tell him and he was very pleased. "It is a most gentlemanlike college", he said in stately approval.

John had been entered as a "commoner". There were different ranks amongst the undergraduates. If you were clever and rather poor, you could win a scholarship and be a "scholar". The ordinary undergraduate was a "commoner" and, if you could pay higher fees and lay claim to being a gentleman or a titled person, you could hold rank accordingly. The scholars usually worked quite hard, the commoners worked a little, and the high-ranking undergraduates worked hardly at all. There were not many who thought of Oxford as a shrine of holiness and learning. They thought of it as a place where young gentlemen usually spent a few years.

John came up to Trinity in the following June because he could not get vacant rooms earlier. Oxford was even lovelier than before, surrounded by its summer green, and the new undergraduate was even more excited than he had been on his first coming there. He went to buy his gown, and the tailor, seeing how new and young his customer was, managed to sell him one that was too big. "You'll grow into it, sir," he said, very cunning and smooth. Back over the road to Trinity, and how odd it seemed that "going home" should be going there!

Almost immediately there was a knock at his door. Another undergraduate had called to show this new one the ropes. He was a pleasant-faced young man, called John William Bowden.

"Mr Short, our Tutor, sent me to show you the College," he said. "Have you met him? He is a great person for work, you know."

And Bowden, who was no idler himself, looked at the new Trinity man and wondered how he was going to like having his noble nose put to the grindstone by Mr Short. Young Newman listened and rejoiced. A strict Tutor would be just the thing! He was licking his lips at the thought of getting down to work.

But now, said his mentor, they would go into Hall to dine. They went in and took their places with the other undergraduates. Some of them (you could sort them out by the cut of their gowns) were commoners like John himself, and a few were scholars; a few grand youths were noblemen and had special gold tufts on their caps, and some were gentlemen commoners. The "tufts" and the gentlemen were mostly loud and proud, making a lot of themselves and tossing down their drink. John left them alone and concentrated on his surroundings. The hall was mellow and beautiful, with the candlelight winking on the dark polished wood, on the brightness of silver and the dull gleam of pewter. And the food! Really, he had never seen such a dinner.

At dinner [he wrote in his first letter home] I was much entertained with the novelty of the thing. Fish, flesh and fowl, beautiful salmon, haunches of mutton, lamb, etc. fine strong beer; served up in old pewter plates and misshapen earthenware jugs. Tell Mama there were gooseberry, raspberry and apricot pies.

He also wrote that he intended to get all the information he could respecting the books he ought to study. He could not find Mr Short, however, when he tried to get his reading list. Since it was so very late in the term, Oxford was emptying fast. He called on the President and waited an hour and a half in the parlour before he discovered that the great gentleman was out. He tried again, was more successful and presented his difficulty. "Well, Mr Newman," said the President, kind and courteous, but inwardly surprised at a request for work, "I leave all such questions to the Tutors."

Now that was all very well, but Tutors were rare beings, at that moment. How to find one? The earnest John puzzled over the problem as he walked in the Parks, and fortune favoured him, for as he turned homewards he saw one of the Tutors, in his top-boots, riding out. It was now or never, so he sprinted into the road and stopped the horse. The Tutor, like the President, was inwardly amazed but outwardly polite, and he directed this keen youth to another Tutor in the College, who supplied him with what he wanted.

In those first, strange weeks, John Henry Newman was greatly helped and cheered by having John William Bowden as his friend. The two were very close to each other all their undergraduate days. They worked together, went walking and boating together, were in and out of one another's rooms in term-time, and stayed with each other in the vacations. Christian names were never used among the young gentlemen of 1817. "Newman" and "Bowden" were the names they used, and they spoke them so often that Bowden stuck in the groove; in later years, when he was married, he sometimes called his wife "Newman".

When he had once settled down, life at Oxford was full of happiness for Newman. The worship of God, beauty and learning and friendship: all that he valued most were there. He noticed how the snapdragon grew on the walls of Trinity outside his rooms, and he took the flower as a kind of emblem. The snapdragon is a sturdy plant, and when it has thrust its roots into the soil it goes on flowering in its plot year after year. His residence in the University would be like that. Oxford was his chosen place and he was thrusting his roots into its soil. There he would stay.

And what was the strict Mr Short doing now that he had young Newman for a pupil? He was rubbing his hands with glee. "Oh, Mr Newman," he said when he met his pupil's father, "what you have given us in your son!" He could hardly find work hard enough for the young man, particularly in mathematics.

23

"I know all about multiple, superparticular, submultiple, subsuperparticular, subsuperpartient of the lesser inequality, sesquilateral, sequiquintal, supertriquartal and subsuperbitertial."

said John in one of his letters home, and Mama did not know whether to rejoice in pride at his cleverness or wish that she could hear instead that he was eating his fill of those good nourishing joints and fruit pies served in Trinity Hall.

Mr Short entered John Henry Newman for a scholarship examination and he won the scholarship with ease (so he never grew into that commoner's gown after all). There was a rising hope in Trinity that this young man would do them credit and gain high honours in his final examinations. Some of the colleges at this time were stirring and looking about them and thinking it was time their undergraduates gave themselves to serious study instead of getting drunk regularly at rowdy wine-parties. Trinity had not scored any academic success yet, but it was a college that was rousing itself from the old slackness.

It was another college that had the name for thought and learning—Oriel College. There the dons, at any rate, did not drink so much wine since it befuddled the intellect. They drank tea instead. Rowdy youths amused themselves by whacking on the lodge gates and shouting, "Porter, does the kettle boil?"

Perhaps it was because Trinity was not used to preparing candidates for distinction in the Final Schools that good Mr Short proved so inefficient when it came to teaching his promising pupil. He did not point out the useful books to read, so that Newman read more widely than wisely. And he did not think to issue any warnings against overdoing things. Newman rose very early, lit his own fire, and then "fagged" at his books nearly all day. For twenty weeks before the examinations he worked twelve hours a day, regularly. If he read only nine hours one day, he would read fifteen the next.

As the time drew near, he grew tired and depressed. They said he would get the highest honours, a Double First in Classics and Mathematics and sometimes he was desperately anxious to succeed. At other times he was remorseful about such ambitions. He prayed hard, not that he would succeed, but that he would not get any honours if they were to be the least cause of sin to him.

In fact, when Final Schools came, he broke down completely and failed to get his First. He was not placed at all in Mathematics, and in Classics he was placed "below the line"; in modern terms, he got a Third. The moral of his undergraduate days seems to be, in fact, that it is a bad idea to work too hard.

He wrote a sad letter home, hating to disappoint his parents, and they wrote a kind and cheering letter in reply. Then, curiously enough after such an experience in the Schools, Newman became calm and cheerful and did not lose confidence in his own powers. His scholarship still had some years to run so he need not leave Oxford, but if his dream of a permanent place in the University was to be realised, he would have to become a don, a Fellow at one of the colleges. A Fellow is one of the senior men responsible for the running of a college, chosen to uphold the dignity and the scholarship of the place. It was not likely on the face of it, that any college would want a young man with a Third Class degree, but he did not give up hope. First he happily spent some months in dabbling in a good many subjects that interested him, mineralogy and geology and music. The family must have smiled when they heard that he was not only playing his violin but was turning composer: "I am glad to be able to inform you that Signor Giovanni Enrico Neandrini has finished his first composition. The melody is light and airy and is well supported by the harmony."

Then he calmly astonished his friends by announcing his resolve to try for a Fellowship—at Oriel, the most exclusive college of them all! The Fellows of Oriel were some of the most brilliant men of the day and there was no greater academic honour in Oxford, at that time, than to be counted among them. Some people thought him rash and bold, but there was no harm in his trying.

So it was examination time again, and Newman wrote his papers in Oriel Hall. It was April, 1822. By the third day of the examination the examiners had read the papers already done and they sent across to Trinity to find out more about the candidate John Henry Newman because they were interested in him. Mr Short thought this was a most hopeful sign, and he sent for Newman. He had been questioned by the Oriel examiners in confidence, and he could not tell his pupil how he was doing, but he felt there was no harm in having a friendly word.

Mr Short was at an early dinner when Newman called. He glanced up from his plate of lamb cutlets and did not like his pupil's looks. The poor young man was pale and strained, and could obviously do with a square meal. Mr Short behaved in a most sensible and helpful way. He made Newman sit down and partake of the lamb cutlets, nicely served up with fried parsley, and then he spoke encouragingly about the examination. Newman, who had half thought of giving up, was warmed and heartened. After dinner he went away quite cheerful and ready for the next part of the examination. Mr Short settled back in his chair, well satisfied with his dinner and his timely intervention in young Newman's affairs. He had a strong hope that those lamb chops had been eaten to very good purpose.

Sure enough, on April 12th, the Oriel butler was sent over to Mr Newman's lodgings in Broad Street with an important message. He found the young man playing his violin. He delivered the message in the usual style for such occasions—"I am afraid, sir, I have disagreeable news to announce. It is that Mr Newman has been elected Fellow of Oriel, and his immediate presence is required there." Newman did not think his style of address was very funny; in fact he thought it was cheeky. Anyway, such great news struck him with stiffness and shyness. He just said,

"Very well," and went on fiddling. The butler lingered in the doorway, and then asked if he had made a mistake and come to the right person. "It's all right," muttered the new Fellow of Oriel, still sawing away on his fiddle. So the butler went away, rather confused.

The minute he had gone, Newman leapt to life, put away his instrument and scudded down the Broad towards Oriel. All the tradespeople popped out of their doorways to see him, since they knew where he was hurrying, and why (for news travels fast in Oxford). The bells were rung from three towers to celebrate his success. He had to pay for those bells, afterwards.

All the men at Trinity were simply delighted and rushed up and down the staircases shouting the good news. One young man nearly had his door broken down by an excited friend.

At Oriel, Newman was kindly received by the Provost and the Fellows. He knew many of them by name, because they were famous for their learning, and he was most abashed to find that he was expected to call them by their names, without a polite "Mister". It seemed unbelievable that he should be called "Newman" by these great men, and have to say "Hawkins", "Whately" and "Keble" in return.

He wrote in his Journal, "Friday, April 12th. I have this morning been elected Fellow of Oriel. Thank God. thank God."

He kept the day as an anniversary ever afterwards. It was a great triumph, "of all days, most memorable".

3 – Oriel

The Fellows of Oriel were, of course, very interested to see how the new member of their Senior Common Room would make out. But they could get nothing from him. He was dumb with shyness and looked as though he would like to shrink through the floor when anyone spoke to him. They began to wonder if they had picked a dud after all.

The Provost (the Head of Oriel), whose name was Copleston, sometimes felt thoroughly irritated by young Newman's shyness and unhandy ways. One day at dinner he called crossly down the table, "Mr Newman, we do not serve sweetbreads with a spoon! Fetch Mr Newman a blunt knife!" Newman felt sure every eye was fixed on him; he wanted to rush away and never see a dish of sweetbreads again.

On another occasion, however, Copleston felt moved to be kind and complimentary. He saw Newman on one of his solitary walks, and as he drew close to him he noticed how gravely attentive the young man's face was. Was he thinking something out? Or was he praying? He was certainly not walking idly, letting his mind go blank. Copleston bowed and made a Latin compliment. "Nunquam minus solus quam cum solus", he said. "You are never less alone than when you are alone, Mr Newman."

But these forever solitary walks could not go on. Someone must try to get Newman out of his shell. The Oriel Fellows asked the Reverend Mr Whately to see what he could do for him. Now Whately, one of the best known Fellows of Oriel, was a loud-voiced, rough-mannered man who cared little for appearances. You could see him most days with his dogs, Bishop and Sailor, striding through the Parks, throwing sticks, the dogs barking and Whately shouting and bawling. He was a great talker. One day he was sitting in a lady's drawing room on a nice little chair with spindly legs. He lurched about, talking all the time, and a cracking noise was heard. The poor lady saw one of the legs of her chair coming off. Whately just reached for the severed leg, tossed it on the sofa, moved to another chair, and went on with what he was saying. He had revolting table manners, and no one (not even the Provost) could shout at him. He would have served the sweetbreads with a pick and shovel if he had liked.

Whately was a clever man, and a kind one, well used to teaching young men to give as well as they got in an argument. He said he would lick Newman into shape, and the young man would have to be "like the dogs of King Charles' breed, who can be held up by one leg without yelling". No one could mind this treatment from Whately because he was really friendly, for all his loud sharp ways; he was a "bright June sun tempered by a March northeaster". A silent, shy young man would be happy in his company because he would not feel that he had to speak; it was so evident that Whately could do enough talking for two. Then, in time, the silent one would speak out of his own accord. The plan worked. Whately took Newman out walking and riding; he got him to talk, he sharpened his wits and made him think for himself. He reported to the other Fellows that they had made no mistake in electing Newman. "He is the clearest-headed man I know," said Whately.

Another Fellow of Oriel, the Reverend Mr Hawkins, also befriended Newman, and helped to open his mind, and so did yet another man, not from Oriel this time, but from Christ Church, Dr Lloyd, the Regius Professor of Divinity. Lloyd heard that Newman was an Evangelical, and he disliked evangelical notions, but when he met the young man he found he liked him, even if he did not agree with his ideas. He gave lectures to a small group which included Newman, and they learned a great deal from Dr Lloyd, although they had to put up with his odd ways. He lectured in a mock-pompous style, and every so often he would burst out into loud laughter, or pick on one of the class and tease him. He pounded up and down as he lectured, asking questions and taking snuff. Very often he stopped when he got to Newman, roared a question at him and dodged at him as though he was going to cuff his head or box his ears. You had to look lively in Dr Lloyd's lectures. All these friends were clergymen and, indeed, it was usual for the college Fellows to be ordained in the Church of England. Newman did not do things just because they were usual; he made up his mind to become a clergyman not in order to fit in with Oxford ways, but in order to serve God.

He was ordained in 1824 and became the curate of St Clement's, a parish that lay on the outskirts of Oxford, just over Magdalen Bridge. He went on being a Fellow of Oriel, of course, and he had pupils to teach as well. The parish kept him pretty busy. He visited his parishioners regularly, and they thought him a nice young gentleman. A new church was being built, and Newman collected the money for it, though he did not have anything to do with choosing the design. It was not a handsome church, and people rudely called it "the boiled rabbit". You can still see it, in rather pale stone, with its "ears" sticking up from the flat meadows that surround it. If he was in doubt about his new duties he would consult his good friend Hawkins, who was the Vicar of St Mary's Church, and a most conscientious clergyman. They took an evening stroll together and then finished their talk over a cup of tea from the famous Oriel teapot.

Newman was learning so much from his friends. Sometimes they introduced new ideas into his mind, and sometimes they stimulated him to new ideas of his own. He would stride out, in the afternoons, for a rapid walk to Iffley or Shotover, or some other pleasant village or country landmark, or he would sit in his room at Oriel in the evenings, and his mind would be working like a dynamo.

He now felt a change in his religious opinions. When he had been converted at fifteen years old, his teacher, Mr Mayers, had brought home to his heart the great truths about Our Lord. He would be everlastingly grateful for that, and, please God, he would never break that direct personal contact with Him. But he was sure now—and he had always had his doubts—that certain Evangelical notions were wrong. He laid aside the Evangelicals' teaching as a person might take off a coat that had never really fitted.

He was sure now that it was wrong to rely too much on the moment of conversion. No, the important moment was when a person received grace in his baptism and became a child of God and a member of the Church. The Church, he now thought, was of the greatest importance. It was the Kingdom of God, founded by Christ himself to bring his grace and truth to all men. It began with the Apostles, and would last for all time.

When he was very young, Newman must have loved the Bible's account of God's "walking in the garden in the cool of the day" with Adam his friend—long ago in the fresh dawn of the world, before man sinned. He too walked alone with God, so intensely aware of their two selves, himself and his Creator, that everything else seemed shadowy. The picture was a true one, but now he had another picture in his mind. He thought of St John's vision of the Church Triumphant, the City of God, shining with glory like a most precious stone, a City that had no need of light because its light was the Lamb of God. The Christian life, and Heaven itself, was to live in the love of God, alone with God Alone, but it was also to be joined with the whole company of God's people. Did he perhaps begin to have the picture of the City in his mind when he saw its faint earthly image before him—the city of Oxford with its shining towers, the city that proclaimed "The Lord is my Light"?

31

He had fierce arguments about the nature of the Church and about many other points of doctrine with his brother Frank. Frank had come up to Oxford too, and was doing very well (in fact he got the brilliant First that his brother failed to get) and just as John Henry was becoming less of an Evangelical, Frank was becoming more of one. Both brothers had fierce tempers when they felt strongly about anything, and they sometimes had great rows. John was bitterly sorry afterwards for his hot words. No one knows what Frank felt afterwards, but the chances are that he was not particularly sorry for his bad temper against his brother. He went on keeping a grudge against him all his days.

Now why should it be Frank who followed John to the University, and not Charles, who, after all, was next in age? The truth was that Charles would never have done any work at Oxford; in fact, he hardly did any work of any kind, wherever he was. He was a great trial to his family. They got him a job, and within a few weeks he had given it up and was busily writing to his employers a most pompous letter saying how badly he had been treated. So then another job had to be found for him, and again everyone (according to Charles) was in the wrong except Charles Newman. The kindest thing that can be said about him is that he must have been a little cracked in the head.

Poor Mr Newman was sometimes very vexed with his sons. Charlie was a failure and Frank had picked up those dratted Evangelical notions. Mr Newman was an easy-going man who only liked religion in moderation. He was fretted beyond endurance whenever Frank or John talked about "being saved", and when they looked solemn or refused to go to the theatre or write letters on Sunday. John was the most satisfactory son. He was doing well for himself, he was not such a strict Evangelical as Frank, and he was marvellously good to his family when times were hard. He even paid all Frank's expenses at Oxford.

Mr Newman deserved sympathy and patience when he

32

was short-tempered, for he was always harassed by business affairs. Worry at last broke his health, and John was summoned home in the summer of 1824 because of his father's grave illness. He reached home just in time; his father was dying. When it was all over, John wrote in his Journal:

That dread event has happened. Is it possible? O my father, where art thou? I got to town Sunday morning. He knew me; tried to put out his hand and said "God bless you!" Towards the evening of Monday he said his last words. He seemed in great peace of mind.

For years the Newman family had relied a great deal on the eldest son. Now it was even more his responsibility to look after his mother and sisters. John squared his bony shoulders and determined that he would do everything he could for them. Mrs Newman had some money of her own, but sometimes she needed more, and then he supplied it. He cast up the accounts for her, and settled any business matters she might have. For years he had helped to educate his sisters. They were intelligent, bookish girls, but they had no governess, and studied by themselves at home. John kept them well supplied with lists of books to read, and with notes and suggestions.

Harriett and Jemima and Mary wore their hair brushed into two bunches of ringlets, as the fashion was. It is a style that makes a young lady look rather like a spaniel with long, dangling, curly ears. Harriett was like a little, pretty sharp-voiced dog, sometimes given to snaps and yaps. Jem was more like a heavy clumber spaniel, large-eyed, kind and rather slow.

There are no comparisons that will serve for Mary—she was just herself. Mary Newman was a darling. She was good but never dull, clever and hard-working but never over-solemn. She put a gay sparkle on all she did or said or wrote. John loved her very dearly. Sometimes he thought about the extreme loveliness of her character and his own great affection for her, and a little shiver of presentiment came over him. Was it possible that she could live on to delight people? He was afraid he loved her too well, and he held himself back from enjoying her dear society to the full.

Mary loved, admired and respected her eldest brother—but for all that, she teased him whenever she felt inclined. She wrote delightful letters, written fast enough to make her quill pen splutter. She chattered on as though her brother was only the length of the room away. Once she wrote to him: "How I long to see you, nice creature! I can fancy your face. There it is looking at me."

Thoughts of that affectionate home circle warmed Newman's heart whenever he felt a little downcast and fatigued. He worked dreadfully hard, studying, writing, teaching, preaching, looking after his parishioners and students. In 1825 Whately became Principal of Alban Hall, a hall of residence for some of the undergraduates, and he appointed Newman as his Vice-Principal. As a matter of fact, Newman was also the Bursar, the Chaplain and the Dean, a kind of Lord High Everything Else, and there were mountains of work for him to do.

Gone were the days of Newman the young, shy Fellow of Oriel. He had come right out of his shell and was leading a most successful life. However busy he was, though, he did not neglect his spiritual life. He prayed fervently, he noted carefully in his Journal his resolutions, and with scrupulous honesty he put down his temptations and his sins. You would hardly think that the Devil could deceive him and put a dark cloud between him and the light of God he was following so zealously. The Devil did not, in fact, quite manage it, but he very nearly did, with a subtle and deadly temptation. Newman was beginning to fancy himself as a clever young Fellow of Oriel; he was tempted to think that it was better to be clever than to be good. It was the same temptation that had befallen him in his schooldays.

In those days he was saved from his own pride by being sick and lonely and worried in his last weeks at school.

35

The grief turned to a blessing for him when Mr Mayers and his teaching came to him. Now again God saved him by giving him sorrow. Afterwards he saw quite clearly how he had been rescued, and though it was a great grief that struck him down this time, he was honestly grateful. The affliction came in two forms; he met sickness and bereavement.

4 – Parting from Friends

In 1826, Newman was made an official Tutor of Oriel, and next year he had the important job of Public Examiner. So again he went along to the Examination Schools where he had broken down at his own examination seven years before. A dismal and humiliating thing happened: he fell ill again and had to leave the building, unable to continue.

He went to bed with a dreadful, throbbing headache, feeling as though his eyes were twisting round. The doctor looked grave and said he had "a determination of blood to the head arising from over-exertion of the brain, with a disordered stomach". He was certainly not fit to go on with his Oxford work, so he stayed with some friends for a week and then went down to his family who had rented a house at Brighton.

It was sad, of course, that John had had such a painful reason for a holiday, but it was very pleasant to have him, and he recovered well after a rest. At the beginning of January, the Newman family had two young ladies to stay. One of them, Miss Maria Giberne, has left us an account of the visit, with full details. Maria was a handsome, dark girl, with very strict Evangelical principles. Frank was deeply in love with her, but she was not so keen about Frank. She was friendly with the Newman sisters, particularly with Mary, though she thought them rather worldly. They made jokes continually, and never once did she hear them discussing all the details of their soul's progress, or praying out loud. It was very surprising, she thought, in a good Christian family. She was fascinated by their eldest brother. He was supposed to be very religious, but she could not draw him out to talk, or pray, either. Still, she enjoyed their company, despite her doubts of their earnestness.

On January 4th they had a little dinner party. It was a good dinner, with turkey to eat. Mary Newman looked pale and distressed, with great circles under her eyes. She hesitated to leave the table for fear of spoiling the party, but at last she had to go out. Mrs Newman followed her, and came back later, looking perturbed, and saying, "John, I think we must send for the doctor; Mary is very ill."

John said, half-jokingly, trying to lighten his mother's worry for a moment, "Yes, Mother, and don't forget his fee!"

The guests went out the next day. They made polite enquiries, of course, before they went, and though they were sorry for Mary and her family, they did not feel great alarm. When they got back in the evening, John asked them into the empty parlour and told them that the doctor had taken a serious view of Mary's case. Maria Giberne's mind was an odd jumble of thoughts. She was sorry about Mary, and she was also sorry for herself, because she had just had an unpleasant hour at the dentist. She was interested to watch John, who was exercising a great deal of self-control. He looked straight at the fire as he spoke, he kept his hands still and his voice steady, but his face was white, and he could hardly keep his lips from quivering. Maria asked him to pray with them for his sister's recovery. "Now", she thought, "he will show whether he is a good clergyman or not." She was shattered with honest remorse and grief by his next words, "I must tell you that she is dead already."

The death of Mary was, he wrote later that year, "the

heaviest affliction with which the good hand of God has ever visited me". But a blessing and comfort came in the strong feeling that he had of his sister's abiding presence. Just as she had strongly imagined that her brother was near, although they were separated, and could gaily write, "There you are!" so he felt her to be near him still. When he was lying in his bed at night he fancied her there. When he rode about the Oxford countryside "a solemn voice" seemed to speak from the trees and hills. It was Mary's voice. Often he felt that all the world that he saw before him was much less real than the spiritual life that lay beyond it. "What a veil and curtain this world of sense is! Beautiful, but still a veil."

There was little time, though, for sad brooding. Newman had to go back to his Oxford work. Things were moving briskly there, and promotion was the order of the day. Dr Lloyd had become Bishop of Oxford. When he was installed, he wore a great bishop's wig, and he looked so extraordinary in it that it was thought he had put it on back to front! Newman, as we know, had been made a Tutor of Oriel, and he had new and grave responsibilities.

In 1828 other changes came about. Copleston ceased to be Provost of Oriel, and the Fellows had to vote for a new Head for their College. Some of them voted for John Keble, a very good, intelligent and attractive person, but Newman cast his vote for the other candidate, who was his old friend Hawkins. If they were out to elect someone for an angel's place, said Newman, Keble was the one to have, but if they wanted a good Provost, Hawkins would be a better choice. Hawkins was, in fact, elected.

This election meant that someone had to be found to succeed Hawkins as Vicar of St Mary's. The Church of St Mary the Virgin is a lovely, dignified building, standing in the High, only a stone's throw from Oriel. It has a fine porch, with two large twisted pillars and a statue of Our Lady at the top.

Newman was appointed as the new vicar. He had the local shopkeepers as his parishioners, and he also had the task of preaching to members of the University on certain occasions because St Mary's was the University Church. It had stood there, in the most famous street in Oxford, for centuries, its massive building and its soaring spire proclaiming that the University had been built as a shrine of religion as well as learning. Every term the most grave and reverend dons went there in procession, in full academic dress, to represent the University at its public worship. Famous preachers had spoken from its high pulpit. It was indeed an honour to become the vicar there.

So now Newman had two important posts—he was Fellow and Tutor of Oriel and he was Vicar of St Mary's. He was well satisfied with such a place in the University, not just because it was an important place, but because he felt he would now have great opportunities for helping souls to God.

When Hawkins had been Provost for a little time, Newman began to feel rather uneasy. Hawkins had always been a careful, formal man, but now that he was in a powerful position he was becoming stiffer and more snobbish. He cared more for "what was done" than what should be done. He showed a great fondness for the noblemen. He used to extend two fingers to shake hands with an ordinary undergradute, but he gave his whole hand to a tuft. One term he was rather perplexed when it came to greeting one of his Oriel undergraduates. The young man had been a commoner, but he had inherited a title in the vacation, and when he turned up in his silk gown and his gold-tufted cap Hawkins felt shy about giving him the whole-hand treatment for the first time.

It was usual in Oxford at that time to make great divisions between the different sets of men in the colleges. The Tutors kept themselves aloof from the young undergraduates and the Heads of the Houses kept themselves well apart from the Fellows and Tutors. This pleased Hawkins well. He liked everyone to stay in his social box. He put himself in his box and he shut down the lid, and he expected everyone else to do the same.

Now Newman worked on very different principles. As a new Tutor he had been working hard to change Oriel because he felt that there were far too many gentlemen commoners lounging about. He had no use for young gentlemen who came up to Oxford just to drink and hunt. New brooms have stiff bristles, and Newman had been sweeping away very fiercely indeed. When he first became Provost, Hawkins was willing to lend his support to Newman and other eager young Tutors. After all, they obviously had the good of the college at heart. It was Newman's way of dealing with the good, hardworking undergraduates that Hawkins disapproved of more.

If a young man came to Newman as a pupil and he showed that he wanted to profit from his time up at Oxford, he was given every possible help. Newman poured out all the treasures of his own rich mind and spirit for him. Very often an undergraduate who wanted to "read for Honours" could not get much help from his Tutor, and he had to pay for private teaching. Newman was well aware of the system of private tutoring. Had he not taken private pupils himself? Whenever money had been needed in the Newman household—for Frank's bills, or for paying Aunt Betsey's debts, or for getting Charlie out of a scrape —a sum could be earned by taking on another pupil. But he had always thought it a shame that the young men had to pay for their teaching like this. Besides, it was a Tutor's responsibility, he thought, to look after his pupils, and to care for their minds and souls.

When Newman was ordained, he had seriously considered becoming a missionary, but he had decided that he could fulfil his vocation as a clergyman by staying at Oriel, for, after all, to teach and guide and influence the young men there was a real work for souls. So Newman's pupils were given every help and encouragement with their work and with their spiritual lives. It was not all study and religion, either, when Mr Newman was around. He made companions of his pupils, took them out walking or riding in the afternoons, had them in for tea and talk or

40

music in the evenings, and even had them with him in the vacations. He was entertaining as a talker; it was said, for instance, that no one got more out of a newspaper than Newman. He was liked and respected by these young men. They found him a real friend.

Now Hawkins expected Tutors to do some teaching in formal classes and lectures, and then leave the undergraduates alone. "Leave them alone" was the cry amongst many of the senior men at Oriel, and sometimes this meant that great wrong was done as a result. For one thing, the rule of the college was that all undergraduates should attend the Communion service at stated times. They had to go, whether they were prepared to take the Sacrament devoutly or not, and no one cared further than that about the matter.

This was the first time that Newman was faced with the painful choice between pleasing one's friends and following one's conscience. However, he was quite clear about what he had to do. He was not treating his pupils in a certain way just because he liked to do so, but because this was the only way he could do his duty as a clergyman. There was nothing for it but to defy Hawkins, and Newman hated this, for Hawkins was a valued friend. It had been hard to lose his sister, but at any rate she was close to him in spirit, and there had been no shadow of disagreement between them. Oxford friends were not so dear, but it was very painful to lose them through a serious difference of opinion.

Newman could no longer be a close friend of Hawkins, and he was slipping away from Whately too. Whately, good and kind as he was, was a "Liberal" in his opinions —that is, he was a person who valued intelligence more than goodness. And Newman had proved on himself how false and wrong that position was. He said of these friends : "They have come, they have gone; they came to my great joy, they went to my great grief. He who gave, took away."

Mercifully, there were some new friends at hand.

5 — New Friends

Newman was not the only young Tutor of Oriel who took the view that there were things wrong in the system there. Another Tutor who had been appointed about the same time was a young man called Hurrell Froude, and he and Newman had much in common. Froude said that there was a great deal too much "donnishness and humbug" about the place, and they had better put it down.

Hurrell Froude was an eager, bright-eyed, lanky young man, chock-full of intelligence and enthusiasm. He had been a pupil of John Keble and admired him tremendously. He might well have respect and gratitude for Keble, because it was he who had gently won Froude to the service of God, and encouraged him to channel his considerable energy and tame his wild spirit in the pursuit of holiness.

His big hatred was for Pharisees, and he would not tolerate "humbug" in himself any more than he would in any one else. There was nothing conventionally pious in the way Froude went about things. Like Newman, he encouraged his pupils to go out with him, but Froude's pupils had to be ready for some really tough exercise. Even when Newman was a boy at school he would go off quietly with his book and curl up somewhere to read or write while the other boys were roaring or rushing about with bats and balls, but Froude, at school and after school, was a great outdoor person. He loved riding, sailing and skating, and he took his pupils out to share his hobbies. He would even join them when it came to climbing back over the college walls late at night. (Hawkins would have been stricken with horror if he had seen a Tutor shinning over the wall.) He had a bright, sharp wit, and a very attractive way with him. Harriett Newman called him "that bright and beautiful Froude". Underneath all this activity, this wit and charm, he had a most serious purpose. Holiness was his aim, and he went straight at it, knocking down the obstacles, hitting hard at his own faults and human weaknesses. Secretly, very secretly, for he was not going to flaunt his religion like a Pharisee, he prayed for long hours, and kept strict fasts.

Newman had known Keble, Froude's hero and friend, for years, but he had not known him intimately. When Newman had first come up to Oxford he was walking down a street one day with his undergraduate friend, Bowden. Bowden nudged him and said in tones of awe, "There's Keble." Newman looked at him with respect. Keble was known for his cleverness and his goodness. He had a brilliant University record, but he chose to spend his time as the parson of a quiet, country village because he thought that serving God so was better than striving for high positions. When Newman became a Fellow of Oriel, he marvelled to think that the great Keble, also a Fellow of Oriel, would be his companion, and he wrote to tell Bowden of his feelings. All the same, he and Keble had not been close friends. Keble liked John Henry Newman, but he did not approve of his views. Was he not an Evangelical and something of a "Liberal", a follower of Whately? Such people, thought Keble, were not thoroughly loyal to the Church of England, and the Church was all-in-all to Keble. Froude had seen, however, that Newman's views had changed, and he brought his two friends together. He used to say that he was like the murderer who could boast of one good action in his life—his good deed had been bringing Keble and Newman together.

There was another Fellow of Oriel, renowned for his learning, who was increasingly friendly with Newman too. His name was Pusey—Edward Bouverie Pusey. Newman described him like this:

His light curly head of hair was damp with the cold water which his headaches made necessary for comfort; he walked fast with a young manner of carrying himself, and stood rather bowed, looking up from under his eyebrows, his shoulders rounded and his bachelor's gown not buttoned at the elbow but hanging loose at his wrists. His countenance was very sweet and he spoke little.

Newman, when he first knew him, was a little deceived by his quietness and humility, and wished he were more religious. But when he knew him better he was ashamed of his own first, rather self-righteous judgment. Pusey, he discovered, was a really holy person. He was very serious and very learned. He was not very old; like Newman, he had learned a great deal and risen in the world in a very short time. For all this, however, and for all his "young manner of carrying himself" it is difficult to think of Pusey except as a rather elderly man, just as it is impossible to think of Froude as anything but a young one. If we play Mary Newman's trick, shut our eyes and try to make a little, vivid picture in our minds, there is Froude legging it over the college wall, or striding in the open country, but Pusey is walking along an Oxford path with his shoulders bowed and his gown sleeves flapping. He has a headache, poor, good Pusey, and he is thinking over some weighty matter.

Newman had another group of friends, too, acquired about the same time. The names of some of them were Athanasius, Leo, Ambrose, Cyril, Basil, Gregory Nazianzen, John Chrysostom, Augustine, Jerome, Clement, Ignatius, Justin, Irenaeus, Polycarp and Cyprian. They were all saints—the Doctors and Fathers of the early Church.

In the early centuries of the Church, dreadful heresies had come forth like large and scaly dragons, and these saints attacked them vigorously with the weapons of learning and holiness. They were great champions of truth, and the tomes of theology they had written were full of interest to Newman. He began to read them systematically.

He got Pusey to send him some Folio copies of the

Fathers' writings from Germany when he was studying there. He was simply delighted when they arrived and he could arrange them on his shelves. They were splendid fellows, and so cheap!

He steeped himself in their thought, and he began to feel himself thoroughly at home in those early centuries. Sometimes when he lifted his head from his book, he would blink and rub his tired eyes; it was hard to think himself back to nineteenth-century Oxford. If St Augustine or St John Chrysostom had turned up in his Oriel rooms, Newman would not have had to make any preliminary conversation to get to know him. He would have launched straight into an eager conversation about some interesting point of doctrine, just as he would have done with Froude or Pusey.

He wrote a book about the great Council of Nicaea in the fourth century when the Arian heretics were condemned. The work was called *The Arians of the Fourth Century*. The more he read of the history of that time, the more fascinated he became. One thing led to another. One early Father, so to speak, introduced him to another, and another. "It was launching myself on an ocean with currents innumerable."

Newman was thrilled by this early history because he saw there the splendours of the early Church.

> The self-conquest of her Ascetics, the patience of her Martyrs, the irresistible determination of her Bishops, the joyous swing of her advance both exalted and abashed me,

he said. He was abashed because he could not help comparing the early Church with the Church of England, the fourth century with the nineteenth. He believed the Church of England to be the descendant of the early Church, a true source of truth and grace. But the picture of one Church was depressingly different from that of the other.

The Church of England was in the grip of a quiet world-

45

liness. There were young men who chose the Church as a safe and respectable profession without thinking too much of the spiritual responsibilities. There were the red-faced hunting parsons who came home after a day in the field to ease off their riding boots and take their rest with a good dinner and a large bottle of port. There were the wealthy Bishops, with their well-fed faces under their great wigs, bowling along in their carriages. There were the careless clergy, thinking little of beauty and decorum in the Church's liturgy, and scurrying through the services in their ill-kept churches.

It was clear that the Church of England would not long enjoy the same safe, privileged position she had had in earlier times. Reformers were murmuring that the Church must be shorn of her revenues and privileges; more seriously, there were anti-Church, free-thinking "liberal" men all over the place, encouraging defiance and rebellion against authority, and even against religion.

Many of the clergy were agitated, of course. A stand must be made. But, as Newman and Froude felt, what was the good of the Church standing firm and claiming her rights if she had forgotten her real titles to authority? If the Church of England would remember that she was a Holy and Apostolic Church, and not rely so much on worldly support and worldly authority, her voice would be listened to. There was need of a second Reformation!

Keble, Froude and Newman put their heads together. They were a formidable trio for any enemies of the Church. You had only to look at them to see that. All three had fine-drawn, rather beautiful faces, with eager eyes. They looked very intelligent, very sensitive, full of earnestness and vigour. They were clever men, and good men too, the right people to begin a spiritual fight.

Who, of the three, was the one who started the idea that they should do battle and begin a kind of second Reformation in England? It is impossible to say. Keble had felt the need first, but he was a quiet man, and perhaps he would never have spoken out if he had not been fired by his brilliant and bold pupil Hurrell Froude; and perhaps Froude would not have been able to do anything if he had not become friendly with Newman who was the greatest man of the three, and the one most capable of running men and movements. On the other hand, Newman would never have felt as he did about the Church if he had not been influenced by Froude—and Froude in his turn, had been influenced by Keble. It seemed indeed that the three were meant to come together to start great things.

Newman was always interested in soldiers' exploits. When the Duke of Wellington's despatches were published he said it made him burn to be a soldier. He could have plotted the field for the spiritual battle that he knew must take place soon, working it out with diagrams or flags on a map. The enemy, of course, were the men who were attacking the Church. On the side of the Church there were many battalions that were more of a weakness than a strength. That was the great work that had to be done—to strengthen the Church and put new life and energy into it!

And so Newman began the great task? No—he went on a long holiday.

The occasion for the holiday was a rather alarming and dismal fact. Froude had not been well for some time; it was thought that his lungs were affected and he would do well to winter in a warm climate. So he and his father, Archdeacon Froude, were going on a tour of the Mediterranean, and they invited Newman to go too.

Froude, of course, tried to indicate that his illness was nothing much (he could not stand fuss), but Newman felt a chill of foreboding. The phrase "his lungs are affected" had a dreadful sound in those days, for no cure was then known for tuberculosis, and many people died from it.

The friendship between Newman and Froude had grown steadily from slow and small beginnings. They had walked and talked together, and met constantly in the Oriel Common Room. Now their friendship was warm and strong; Froude was the dearest of Newman's friends. Was he to die young, snatched away from those who loved him, and snatched away from the Church of England too, at a time when she could ill afford to lose his talents?

Well, there was nothing to be gained from being too fearful and gloomy, and perhaps a Mediterranean tour would restore Froude's health. And there was no good reason why he, Newman, should not join them. A curate could look after St Mary's for him. Ordinarily he would hesitate to go away for some months, because he did not wish to leave his pupils in the lurch, but this problem had been solved for him. Hawkins had said firmly that he disapproved of the methods of Newman and certain other young Tutors; he could not eject them from their Oriel Fellowships, but he could and would stop their supply of pupils. So now Newman was a Tutor with no one to teach. He was quite free to go with the Froudes if he wished.

The prospect was very tempting! He had never been abroad before, and, indeed, he had not had much in the way of a holiday for years. He went to stay sometimes with his friends, with Bowden, for instance, or with an Oriel man called Rickards, and there were times when he relaxed quite gaily. On one of his visits Mrs Rickards saw a funny sight. Newman was sitting patiently in an armchair, and both Rickards children were sitting on him. He had the strange, dazed, mild look of a man deprived of his usual spectacles, because the game was to snatch them from him and then jam them on again. One young Rickards pushed his knee more firmly into Mr Newman's waistcoat, and stuck his spectacles back onto his lovely big nose. There were shouts of laughter. Mrs Rickards wondered if she should interfere, but Newman looked as though he were enjoying the game too, so she wrote to Harriett instead, and described the scene.

But even Newman's holidays were often mixed up with work. The very next day after the spectacles game, Mrs Rickards was saying that "the gentlemen are all together in the larger room employed on the Epistle to the Romans." It does not sound very restful.

Now he had the chance of a holiday on the grand scale. He felt very tired after writing his stiff book on the Arians, and he was ready for new and interesting scenes. Yes, he would go! So in December, 1832, he took the coach down to Falmouth, and embarked on the "Hermes" with Archdeacon Froude and Hurrell.

6 — A Voyage to the Mediterranean

The "Hermes" put out into the Atlantic. The roll of the ship soon sent the Archdeacon to his berth, but Newman was a better sailor than that, and managed to get about. He had a double-berthed cabin, a poky, stuffy place. He lay in the top berth of a morning, listening with amusement to the strange sounds, the creaking of the ship, "like a hundred watchmen's rattles mixed with the squeaking of Brobdingnag pigs", and then the washing of the deck, "half-a-dozen brooms, wish-wash, wish-wash, scrib-scrub, scratching and roaring alternately. Then the heavy flump-flump of the huge cloth which is meant to dry the deck as a towel or duster."

In three days they sighted the Spanish coast. They saw a rocky shore with lines of magnificent mountains behind. The sea was a deep dark blue or purple; as night fell, it brightened and glowed to lilac in a splendid sunset. The sky was a pale orange and then red, and the evening star shone out with its peculiar brightness.

Two more days and they were sailing about a mile from the shores of Portugal and saw the beauty of its shining cliffs. They looked through their glasses and could see the houses and windmills and towers, woods of cork trees and little groups of people, all clear and bright in the southern sunlight. How exciting it all was, and how different from

Oxford, with its spires and towers rising to a pale rain-washed sky. There the silver river ran through a flat, misty landscape, and the colours were delicate and hazy, like those in a fine and faded watercolour. But here the outlines were much more bold, and the colours were rich.

Newman wrote long and chatty letters home, giving all the details of the places he was seeing, and telling all the small bits of information that would interest and amuse his mother and sisters—how the fastening of his new carpet-bag had broken right at the start of his journeyings, how "Harriett's purse" had somehow got itself ripped, and how he was eating his meals with a stolid determination because he believed that was the best way to prevent sea-sickness. He also sent home copies of the poems he had written, for he was busying himself aboard with verse-making.

One long letter went home about Gibraltar, where they were put ashore. There was much to tell, about the rock formations, and the Moorish fortifications, and about having had lunch at Government House.

On they went again, sailing now into the Mediterranean itself. The pleasure and excitement of travel was doubled for Newman now. He was visiting scenes he had met a hundred times before in his industrious reading life. He knew the Bible well, he had read all the Greek and Roman classics, he had delved in ancient history, he had read the Fathers, and so, every moment of his journeying now, the air was thronged with memories. History was all about him:

What has inspired me with all sorts of strange reflections these two days is the thought that I am in the Mediterranean. Consider how the coasts of the Mediterranean have been the seat and scene of the most celebrated empires and events which are in history. Think of the variety of men, famous in every way, who have had to do with it. Here the Romans and the Carthaginians fought; here the Phoenicians traded; here Jonah was in the storm; here St Paul was shipwrecked; here the great Athanasius voyaged to Rome.

They saw Algiers and the track to Carthage, and then a bad time at sea followed for all those on board the "Hermes" for there was a gale severe enough to make even the sailors sea-sick. Newman noted with rueful humour how the complaint was made worse by everything joining in—the chairs and tables, the knives and forks, the beds and bulkheads all lurched about as though they were sick too.

By Christmas Day the travellers were at Malta, but they had to stay in harbour in quarantine for cholera. It was sad to stay aboard and hear the church bells, deep and sonorous, and not to be able to read the service in the house of God on such a holy day.

They could not safely travel on the mainland of Greece because the country was in a state of political turmoil, and was full of revolutionary forces, pirates and bandits. So they cruised about the Ionian Isles, and saw Zante, Patras and Corfu. They sailed by Ithaca, the island of Ulysses, and Newman remembered vividly the time when he was a very little boy and heard the story for the first time, and then played at being Ulysses in the garden at Ham. Corfu was one of his favourite places. He observed its olives and myrtles, orange trees and lovely cypresses, and the surrounding high mountains "of a brilliant white or slate colour, folded in long plaits like a tablecloth artificially disposed along a rising and falling outline, without crease or rumple".

Not a detail escaped his close and delighted observation. He noted in his letters not only the large and obvious splendours, but the little, interesting facts—how the sheep on Corfu were not woolly, but had soft, silky fleeces like hair, and how the cows were like wild ones, with strange necks and backs.

For all the intense enjoyment of travelling, Newman had his times of homesickness. Letters from home were delayed, and he yearned for them so much that his sleep was troubled. "I dream about you all and that letters are brought me; but when I begin to read, they are illegible, or I wake up, as if there were men trying to tell me, and others preventing it." Sometimes he fancied himself back in Oxford, because the ship's bells were "provokingly like the Oriel clock". Sometimes he felt tired of all the turmoil of spirit that came with such exciting experiences, and thought they would be best in memory. He wished that he were safe and quiet in his room at Oriel, with his outer door shut as a sign that he was not at home to visitors, or, as they say in Oxford, "with his oak sported". Oh to be there, shut away, lying full length on the sofa!

Back at Malta they had to spend more time in quarantine in a special lodging called the Lazaretto. To while away the time there, Newman learned Italian and hired a violin. They had an exciting night in the Lazaretto, thinking they heard ghosts. Newman paid for the excitement of sitting up in bed on a cold night listening for Maltese ghosts by catching a very bad cold. Even when their quarantine was over he had to stay in, while the Froudes went out sight-seeing, so he did not see much of Malta.

They saw the "Hermes" put off from there, for they were not to sail in her any more. It was rather melancholy to watch their sea-home disappear over the horizon. It made them feel so very far from England.

Sicily was the next place they visited. Perhaps of all the places he saw, it was Segesta, in Sicily, that most seized Newman's imagination. To see this place, the travellers went through a wild countryside, and came at last to a steep rock rising from a ravine. At the top of the rock was a vast, ruined temple, with great Doric pillars but no roof. All around was silence and desolation. Only the temple bore witness to the time when living men had erected it there, a monument to their power and glory. Their civilisation had vanished away, and there it stood, a splendid ruin. The picture of it remained with Newman. He felt it to have a strange and wonderful power and sig-

"It was Segesta that most seized his imagination"

nificance, and deep in his heart he yearned to see it again. The wild places of Sicily were to draw him like a magnet. In Italy itself Naples was a great disappointment to Newman. He did not think much of the famous Bay, surrounded, he said, "by lumpish cliffs like bolsters". The streets were greasy, and dirty urchins plagued travellers for money. The services in the churches were not conducted with proper reverence, and the priests looked low fellows. In fact, said Newman, the only good reason for going to Naples was to eat the ices.

Rome was no disappointment. It filled Newman's mind with deep and conflicting thoughts. He loved the city, and he feared it too. Rome bore in its ruins, and in the history they spoke of, the marks of God's vengeance. There a corrupt empire had flourished, and martyred the saints, and still Rome was the centre of a corrupt and superstitious religion. Newman had a deep distrust of the Roman Catholic Church. And yet there was so much to love and admire in Rome!

Newman visited the museums and galleries and libraries. He particularly enjoyed Raphael's pictures and gazed for a long time at the faces; they had a strange, unearthly expression, full of simplicity. He visited the countless churches, and felt "quite abased" by the enormous size and dignity and grace of proportion of St Peter's and St John Lateran. Two beauties that he had not thought of before were the mosaics and the fountains. He thought the large fountains in the Piazza of St Peter's like "a graceful white lady arrayed in the finest, most silvery of dresses". And Rome was not only a place of beauty, it was the city of the Apostles and the early saints.

Newman summed up his impressions by saying:

> And now what can I say of Rome but that it is the first of cities and that all I ever saw are but as dust (even dear Oxford inclusive) compared with its majesty and glory.

While they were in Rome, Newman and Froude called on an English priest called Nicholas Wiseman. They found him very agreeable (for all he was a Roman Catholic) but they told him they could not make a second visit to Rome. "We have work to do in England", they said solemnly.

Now the plan was to go back to England by way of France, and after his statement to Wiseman one would expect that Newman would have gone back with the Froudes, as he had originally intended to. But he was filled with a strange obstinacy. It was not really sensible, it was not what everyone expected, it was not even wholly polite to the Froudes—but he was not returning to England yet. He was going back to Sicily for a time.

So the Froudes departed, and Newman retraced his steps. He reached Naples and sat over his dinner. The dishes were all about him, in the Italian style, and he brooded gently over the nearest one, a large dish of young green peas. Here he was, for the first time. alone in a foreign land; he was going to lead a wild life in wild places because he was "drawn by a strange love of Sicily to gaze upon its cities and mountains". Was he doing a mad thing? It might be mad, but he was going to do it.

Naples did not please him any more than it had done before (just like Brighton, he said), but he had an interesting though painful expedition to Vesuvius. He went right inside, and hot cinders got inside his shoes so that he, in extreme discomfort, had to find a grip for his hands, and got them burnt, too, on the hot sides of the volcanic crater.

He bought provisions for his journeyings into the interior of Sicily—a set of cooking utensils, an outfit for making tea, some curry powder, spice, pepper, salt, sugar, tea, ham, cold-cream, a straw hat and a map. His foodstuffs went mouldy in a very short time, so he need not have bothered to get them. Later, at Messina, he hired mules and a servant called Gennaro.

On setting off from Messina I felt amused and almost ashamed of the figure I was cutting. I was chief of a cavalcade consisting of a servant, two mules and several muleteers (though the latter were soon reduced to one, who was to be with us through) and when I happened to catch a sight of my shadow, the thought of my personal equipment, at least as regards my hat and my coat, were still more perplexing. My neckcloth was the only black thing about me, yet black without being clerical.

There is a note of surprise bordering on horror in his description. Here was he, an Oxford don, a clergyman of the Church of England, sitting on a Sicilian mule; he was out of his customary black clothes, and wearing a straw hat. He would hardly be surprised, you feel, to find himself soon with a striped kerchief on his head, large gold rings in his ears and black mustachios on his face.

Letters reached England from Syracuse and Catania giving an account of his travels, and then a great silence fell. The Newman family were left worrying, and wondering whether John had fallen into trouble of some kind. He had.

7 – Illness in Sicily

Late in April 1833, Newman went back from Syracuse to Catania by a long boat called a *speronara*. They had to put back because the wind changed, and so Newman rode from Agosto to Catania on his mule, a dreadful, jolting journey, leaving him more dead than alive. He had had two nights in the open, for a *speronara* has only an awning over an open deck, and he had travelled both ways in one. On previous nights he had not slept very well either, because of the fleas, and he had gone rather short of food because he could not buy much that was palatable in the inns, and his own provisions had not lasted. He had had a rough time, and by now he was in a state of real bodily weakness so that any germ that was coming his way would be able to take hold of him. After a few days rest at Catania, he set out towards Girgenti on the south coast. He struggled on as far as a place called Leonforte.

He felt really ill by this time. His servant Gennaro, who was a seasoned war campaigner, and who knew a thing or two, served his master with camomile tea, and said with a knowing wag of his head that he thought he had a fever coming. "Oh no," said Newman, "it's only a stomach-ache like ones I have had at home. Already I feel myself better." But Gennaro was right. Newman went down with a very serious fever.

He lay on his hot bed at the inn at Leonforte and turned many things over in his mind. It was as though he had to search his heart and sift his conscience and face this illness, which might be to death, as a judgment. He thought of his self-will in opposing Hawkins at Oriel, and his obstinate insistence on making this journey into Sicily, and then he went down even further into his past actions and motives, and saw his own "utter hollowness". The fever was not clouding his mind at that moment; indeed, he felt that he was seeing himself more clearly than ever before. He was sorry and ashamed, and yet he felt he could say in honesty, "I have not sinned against the light".

Then he felt a strong sense of God's protecting love, and he thought perhaps he would not die of this fever because God was keeping him to do some special work for Him.

And then he lay still, not thinking at all about these matters, but quite given up to weakness and fever, counting the stars and flowers on the pattern of his wallpaper, and feeling miserably disturbed by the whining voices of beggars outside the house.

Gennaro thought his master was certainly dying, and having an eye to the main chance, he leaned over him and told him a story of a sick army officer who had left Gennaro all his baggage in his will, and who then recovered (presumably as a direct result of his good action). Unfortunately for Gennaro's chance of the baggage this time, Newman was too ill to catch the drift of the story.

He did give Gennaro Froude's address so that he could write there if Newman were to die. "But I do not think I shall," he murmured. "God has still work for me to do. And I have not sinned against the light."

Gennaro shrugged his shoulders expressively. This poor Englishman was delirious and talking rubbish. It was a pity he hadn't used his breath to dictate a statement about the baggage instead. Well, he would do what he could for him, although he did not think there was much hope. Gennaro was a tough ruffian in some ways, quick to lay hold of a few extras for himself, and having a fondness for strong drink, but he had more virtues than vices. He never stole any of Newman's goods, nor his money, though he had excellent opportunities to do so, and he nursed his master with real devotion.

Newman insisted on riding on from Leonforte, though he was extremely ill. In a queer, hazy, feverish way, he thought that pressing on like that was a token that he wanted to go on in God's way, and if he did this, God would protect him in his going. So it proved, in fact, for he found doctors and a safe lodging in the next town, and the move may have saved his life.

On the way, he felt not exactly thirsty, but choked and oppressed. He sat down by the roadside and ate some fine oranges; they were neither sweet nor tart, but "a fine aromatic bitter". Then he plucked leaves from the trees and ate those. Further on, he felt so ill that he lay down on his cloak in a shepherd's hut, and poor people came in a crowd to look at him. Then he felt a hand on his wrist, feeling his pulse. It was a doctor, who told Gennaro to give the sick man camomile, lemon and sugar.

When he was a little refreshed, they were able to hold him on a mule, and bring him to a place called Castro Giovanni. There they found him a nice comfortable room. Another doctor came (he had moustaches and a harsh voice) and bled the patient. Newman conversed with the doctor in Latin and, even in the extremity of fever, his Latin was more correct than the doctor's.

Gennaro had a difficult time with his patient who was flushed and restless, never keeping still for a moment. He did not worry when Signor Newman was fractious, because he knew the poor man could not help it. Gennaro was beginning to think that there might be some hope after all, because the patient took his medicines so well; it was a hopeful sign. They had a quarrel over the drinks though; Gennaro wanted to give him hot tea.

"The doctor said I was to have cold lemonade, and I shall make a formal complaint that you change the prescriptions," said Newman, rather stately and cantankerous, tossing his bedclothes into a fine state.

He could not bear to have Gennaro away from him for five minutes. If the servant went out of the room he was pursued by a feeble voice calling "Gen-nar-r-o-o-o-o. Gen-nar-r-o-o-o-o!" So he slept in his master's room at night, got in an assistant nurse and, if there was no one else to help him, he asked the man in charge of the mules, who was a great hulk of a peasant, not very suitable for a sickroom. However, he did his best. When Newman had fainting fits, as he very often did, he could best be revived by sniffing aromatic vinegar. The muleteer used to give it him "on great bullet-tips of fingers". Poor Newman lay through the long nights, watching the window for the first streaks of dawn. Soon he was bothered by the loud clanging of the Mass bell from the nearby church. When he complained, Gennaro only shrugged, because he thought Newman was objecting as a heretic. Perhaps he thought his master was rather a fighting Protestant, because one day at Castro Giovanni a priest called to visit him in his sickness, and "Bring him in," said Newman, "and I will dispute with him!"

At last the patient took a real turn for the better. Everyone tried to help on his convalescence. The master of the house hired musicians to play in the next room to soothe and entertain him. One day Gennaro got him up and sat him outside. Newman was still very weak; he felt the sight of the sky to be so piercing that he wept.

Now he was beginning to eat properly again. It was like coming back to life to find such a relish in his food. Gennaro made him nice things to eat: chicken broth, an egg baked in wood ashes, tea and little cakes. Never had food tasted so delicious! Newman coaxed for more cakes like a small child.

A letter from home was sent up from Palermo. He was very anxious to know whether a friend and pupil of his called Rogers had been elected to a Fellowship at Oriel, and he pored over the letter, looking for this bit of news. He tired himself so much over this that he had a rush of blood to the head, though he did not have a serious relapse. Health and strength were really coming back to him now. Even the fleas knew it, and came back in force. They had kept off during his feverish time.

At last he was fit to be moved. Speeches were made and Newman gave presents to his kind helpers. When he was about to leave the inn, he sat down on his bed and burst into tears. Gennaro asked him what was the matter, and again Newman said, "I have a work to do in England".

Gennaro helped him into a carriage, and they went by easy stages to Palermo. By now it was late in May and the flowers were bright and luxuriant. All was in tune with Newman's feelings of reviving life. In Palermo he put up at an inn where the hostess, who was an Englishwoman, was kind and made Newman sago and tapioca to build him up.

By now he ached to be home again, but he could not get a ship, and so he had three tedious weeks waiting for transport. He passed slow days sitting about and going on the water every day to improve his health. Sometimes when he was very weary and impatient, he went into the churches and sat there, and a strange peace fell upon him; he felt strengthened and soothed.

The only interest came with the news that Rogers had

his Fellowship. Newman learnt this in a paper, and it stirred his impatience afresh. What was happening in Oxford? How was the Church of England? What mischief were the "Liberals" doing? He had enjoyed seeing all these historical sites and beautiful scenes abroad, but men were more interesting than scenes, and he was not deeply concerned about men and affairs in these foreign parts. England claimed his thoughts.

Gennaro left him now, and Newman was very grateful to him, and sorry to see him go. He paid his good servant handsomely, but he would not give him his old cloak, though Gennaro said he had a fancy for it. That cloak had been on Newman's bed in his illness and accompanied him in so many travels. It was an old friend now, and he could not bear to part with it.

At last Newman managed to find a ship that he could travel in—an orange-boat bound for Marseilles. And even then he was delayed, for the vessel was becalmed for a whole week in the Straits of Bonifacio.

His yearning to go on and reach home made him think of the first home he remembered—the garden at Ham, where he thought that angel faces were all about him. Perhaps Heaven would be like a return to the glories of early childhood; light would break after the dark journeyings of life, and it would be morning again. Life was indeed a dark journey, but all would be well because God is our light and guide. We are like the Israelites released from Egypt, struggling on through the wilderness towards the Promised Land, weary and homesick, but at peace because God is leading us. "And the Lord went before them by day in a pillar of cloud, to lead them the way, and by night in a pillar of fire to give them light."

And then Newman thought of the lesson he had had in his illness. All would be well, if only men would not trust to false lights made by their own pride and self-will, false and brilliant flashes of their own cleverness. He had learnt to be humble, and in humility he had learned a deep confidence.

He put all these thoughts into a poem which he called "The Pillar of the Cloud". Usually his poems were not very good, for though he was a poet at heart, the making of verse seemed to dry up his imagination. But for once feeling and expression came together, and he wrote the lines which have become famous:

> Lead, kindly Light, amid the encircling gloom,
> Lead Thou me on!
> The night is dark, and I am far from home,
> Lead Thou me on.
> Keep Thou my feet; I do not ask to see
> The distant scene: one step enough for me.
>
> I was not ever thus, nor prayed that Thou
> Shouldst lead me on;
> I loved to choose and see my path; but now
> Lead Thou me on.
> I loved the garish day, and, 'spite of fears,
> Pride ruled my will! remember not past years.
>
> So long Thy power hath blest me, sure it still
> Will lead me on,
> O'er moor and fen, o'er crag and torrent till
> The night is gone.
> And with the morn those Angels faces smile
> Which I have loved long since, and lost awhile.

8 — Home again—to the Oxford Movement

Mrs Newman, Harriett and Jemima had been living near Oxford for some time, renting one house after another, in this village or that. John had ridden out to them frequently, on his mare Klepper, and sometimes he brought his friends and pupils too, so there was plenty of social life for the Newman ladies, and Harriett and Jemima had many a cosy confabulation after these social evenings, upstairs in their bedroom, discussing the young men, and who was most charming and attentive among them.

Now they had settled themselves at a house called Rose Bank at Iffley. This is a pretty village and very convenient for the Newmans because it is not far from Littlemore, and the Vicar of St Mary's, by some curious arrangement, was also responsible for the parish of Littlemore, a rather dreary hamlet not far from the city. Newman loved his second parish, though it had nothing very beautiful about it; perhaps he felt more of a parish priest there than he did at St Mary's. He was delighted to have his mother and his sisters there at hand to do the work that the Vicar's wife would usually do, visiting the sick and poor, embroidering such things as altar cloths, and seeing that the Sunday School children had clean clothes and faces and behaved themselves in church.

They had a pleasant family life at Rose Bank. Often in vacation time, they would congregate in their sitting-room, and John would read to the ladies as they busied themselves with their sewing. He treated them to some good solid instruction, volumes of sermons and chapters from his own *Arians of the Fourth Century*. Mama, presumably, could always concentrate on her stitches if she lost the thread of the argument, or go off into a little reverie about other matters.

Once, when Maria Giberne came to stay, she drew a picture of the Newmans in just such a family group. She had a great talent for drawing, and there were a good many Newman portraits in her collection. Her eyes filled with tears when she remembered how Mary Newman had run to meet her when she arrived on that memorable visit, on that January day. "I am so glad you are here," she had said, "and I hope you will help me with my sketching." And a few days later Maria had used her talent, not to help Mary, but to give her family a likeness of her. She had drawn Mary Newman after death, lying on her bed, with her calm, sweet face, and her dark curls carefully arranged under her frilled cap.

Now Maria sketched them all as they sat together. Jemima was in the front of the picture, on a low stool. A pity, really (thought Maria, as she drew in the outlines), to do dear Jem in profile. She had The Nose, and on her young woman's face it did not look distinguished as it did on her eldest brother's rather rugged countenance, but just large. Mama was in the centre, with a handsome cap with bows on her head; she was busy with her work. Frank was to the right of Mama, rather posed, and looking extremely handsome. Maria looked at his classic features (like John's, but not so much of them) and at his blue eyes, and she looked without a tremor. She could not give her heart to Frank Newman, poor Maria Giberne, because she had a sweetheart in India, who died just before their marriage.

Now to the other side of the picture. She drew in Harriett, very pretty with her multitudinous fair curls in order. John was looking down at her. He had had a haircut, and then rumpled his short, soft hair by putting his hand through it. He looked, with his round spectacles and his beak, like an owl with his head feathers ruffled. Maria was rather proud of her grouping of her picture, with John and Harriett a little apart from the others. John came and looked at her handiwork and smiled at her.

"Why," he said, "you have made Harriett look like a young lady that I am sweet on!"

There had been no John and no Frank to read to the ladies for some time now. On 9th July 1833, however, Rose Bank was humming like a hive of pleased bees. John was home again at last, and Frank turned up too on the very same day. He had been on a missionary expedition to Persia (but it was not a very successful attempt to turn the Persians into Evangelical Christians). Only Charlie was absent from this family reunion; he was off somewhere, spending John's and Frank's money.

Perhaps Mrs Newman would have been glad to keep John at home for a while to cosset him. He looked a little like a cheerful scarecrow and a little like a moulting eagle after his illness and the long fatiguing journey home. He was horribly thin and his hair was falling out. Yet even careful Mama could not have persuaded herself that rest was what he needed now. He was bursting with energy. The fever had left him more vigorous than ever, and he was simply spoiling to begin the work he felt God was keeping for him. Froude had been back for some time, and now he was back too. On with the fight! They had chosen a motto for themselves at this time and it was a significant one—"You shall know the difference now that I am back again". They were the words of that doughty Greek fighter, Achilles.

Newman was back in Oxford again in no time, walking down the familiar streets with his quick, light step, thrusting out his head and travelling at a great rate. He looked so different and so strangely charged with energy that his friends hardly recognised him. He was thinking hard, about the present time, and about the past and about the future.

"The times are evil", he said to himself. And if this present world is evil, why, then the Christian must not hide away but he must be up and doing, fighting in the Lord's wars. Newman always realised that this world is a shadow, compared with the reality of the spiritual world beyond it. But he also knew that this everyday world, here and now, is our battleground. Here we can fight for God. Now is the time to do it.

He looked down the long vistas of the past years to see where history would illuminate the present. He saw certain truths shining out clearly in earlier times, truths that were now in danger of being obscured, though they were meant to shine for ever. He gazed into the fourth and fifth centuries, the times of his beloved Church Fathers. He looked back, too, to the seventeenth century, the time when the Church of England was most sure in its beliefs.

On the wall of many an Oxford college there is a portrait of some learned seventeenth-century clergyman. These grave Divines have billowing lawn sleeves, and they hold a Bible or a Prayer Book in their long, white fingers. They looked down solemnly from the dark frames, and they seemed to ask for help in this hour of peril to the Church of England—their Church, and Newman's too.

Then Newman looked into the future, and his gaze was strangely penetrating. He saw the modern world, ushered in with the Industrial Revolution, busy and powerful and intent on many things, but neglecting God more and more.

And while such an era was coming, the Church of England was wrapped in the grey mists of sleep!

Strangely enough, it was Keble, that mild and patient man, who first raised his voice to call men to a sense of responsibility and present danger. The Government was out to knock at the Church good and hard, and made a start by suppressing ten Anglican bishoprics in Ireland. That was Keble's signal, and he preached against this action of the State in a sermon given at the opening of Assizes on 14th July 1833. It was the very first Sunday after Newman had reached home. He was always a great person for dates and anniversaries, for he loved to cherish in his memory the significant events of life. This day was carefully noted down; it was to be remembered as the start of the religious movement of 1833 and the years that followed—that revival that was known afterwards as the "Oxford Movement".

It was not surprising that it was Oxford that provided the starting-place and the name for such a religious revival, for it was as much a home of the Church of England as it was a University city; in those days every man of importance in the University was also a clergyman.

Other men, though, besides those zealous men from Oxford, Keble and Froude and Newman, had ideas on the subject, and one of them, the Reverend Mr Hugh Rose, summoned a meeting of interested persons at Hadleigh

Parsonage. It was like a meeting of generals just after war has been declared, to plan a campaign.

One method Newman and his friend adopted to spread their ideas was to publish a series of leaflets or "tracts". Everyone was used to religious tracts because they were often written, usually by Evangelicals, and good ladies were fond of peddling them around. Sometimes the Lady Bountiful of a village would take round a basket of nourishing victuals to the poor cottagers, and put in a tract or two to aid their souls as well as their bodies. Very often the tracts would have gloomy but stirring titles: "Repent while yet there is time" or "Sinner, hearken to the voice of the Lord". Such pamphlets had not been used for the sort of dignified and learned expression of ideas that the men of the Oxford Movement were concerned with, but it was a method which might be used with profit. So they did write tracts, and in consequence they were often known as "Tractarians". Newman was ready with his pen. He wrote Tract 1, which was anonymous, short and to the point. He began:

> I am but one of yourselves,—a Presbyter; and therefore I conceal my name lest I should take too much on myself by speaking in my own person. Yet speak I must, for the times are very evil, yet no-one speaks against them.

The Church, he said, was in grave danger, and the clergy must rally round the Bishops, the successors of the Apostles. Even if they did all they should, of course the Bishops might still be in grave danger from the State, and in one way that would be very happy for them, because what could be more blessed for Bishops than to lose all they possessed and be martyred?

The first of these Tracts was printed and priced at 1d. a copy, and Newman and his friends distributed copies to all the clergy they knew, and then rode about the countryside with a bundle of Tracts in front of their saddles, calling on every clergyman's house they came to.

You can imagine the scene at some of the Bishops' Palaces, the Deaneries and Rectories, places where the clergy were going on in the old unspiritual style. Imagine the breakfast-table in a well-off clergyman's house, the heavy silver laid on the snowy damask cloth, the hot food sizzling under the covers, the cold meats on the sideboard. And here is the clergyman himself, already warmed with good coffee, and buttery from muffins, stretching his legs under his solid board, and reaching for his post. First he takes a look at the newspaper, and tut-tuts about the wicked Government (which is his only contribution against the evils of the day) and then he opens the Tract which some-one has sent him.

"Listen to this, my dear!" he says to his wife. "This writer, this cleric (presbyter he calls himself), whoever he is, says of the Bishops, 'We could not wish them a more blessed termination of their course than the spoiling of their goods, and martyrdom.' God bless my soul! The man must be mad! And then there's a lot of stuff about Apostolical Succession. . . ."

Still, part of the Tractarians' objective was gained. People's interest was aroused, people's minds were stirred. There were many who fell in with the ideas expressed in the Tracts which were coming out regularly and fre-quently. Newman wrote No. 2 and No. 3. Keble wrote No. 4, and Bowden, who was not a clergyman, but who was ready to do his part, came in with No. 5. There were plenty more to come. More friends were pressed into service to help with the distribution of Tracts. Even Maria Giberne did her part. She took some Tracts with her when she went out paying afternoon calls, and she would nerv-ously thrust one into the servant's hand at the door, and say, "Give this to your mistress, if you please."

The first Tracts were light weapons, however, compared with some of the later ones which were "like the advance of a battery of heavy artillery"; they were written by Dr Pusey, who joined the Movement a year or two after its start. His Tracts were not piffling little pamphlets, but were thick, solid and learned. He helped in other active ways, by beginning to translate the work of the Fathers, and by holding evening parties at his house, where theological papers were read to improve people's knowledge. These last were not really a success, except as a cure for insomnia, for with the best will in the world the listeners could not help dropping off into a snooze when they had heard a few paragraphs.

Dr Pusey was a great help, though, for his joining in certainly gave the Movement solid respectability. He was a Professor and a Canon of Christ Church, a gentleman of aristocratic family, known widely and respected. When Pusey wrote and spoke, many people took notice. And he was very solid and dependable. He did not rush into the Oxford Movement in five minutes, but once he was in it, he was settled there, and he had an absolutely unshakeable confidence in its aims. Sometimes, now, Tractarians were called "Newmanites" or "Puseyites". It was the second name that stuck, even though Pusey was not the first, nor the most important leader; perhaps this was because anti-Tractarians enjoyed making puns about Puseyites and pus-s-ey cats. *Punch* had a cartoon of the chief men in the Oxford Movement. There is Mother Church in the picture, a severe, governessy, elderly person, with her pus-s-eys at her feet, solemn beasts with human faces.

Many were the visits that Newman paid to the Pusey household. He would go in, and the children, fair, delicate, good little things, would rush to hug him. He would take off his spectacles and try them on their small noses, and then they would sit on his knee while he told them stories. If a solemn religious visitor called and waited outside Dr Pusey's room, he might hear the famous, quiet tones of Newman's voice. And if he did hear the words he would be surprised at them:

Then after a time the old woman became tired of having this broomstick which did all the work for her, so one day she snapped it in two, in a fit of temper. And then—do you know what happened? Both halves of the broomstick began to rush about to help her. One went to draw the water, and the other set about cleaning her cottage . . .

They were a delightful family. Mrs Pusey was a dear person; but a shadow of sorrow lay over that peaceful, loving household because it was feared that she would not live long. Pusey loved his wife with a very great love, and Newman, who lived in his friends' joys and sorrows, felt for him. He knew what it was to love deeply and to fear loss; there had been Mary, and now there was Hurrell Froude who had not recovered his health.

He had gone to live in Barbados, in the West Indies, for the benefit of the sunny climate, and from there he watched the progress of the Oxford Movement and helped it with his prayers. When it became clear that this living abroad would not cure him, he came home to die. That was in 1836.

How sorely Newman missed his friend we cannot really imagine, for he was more sensitive than the ordinary run of men, knowing and appreciating and loving and enjoying more than we shall ever do, and capable, too, of unusual suffering.

Hurrell left two mementoes. Newman was given his dead friend's private journals and papers, and he read there the tale of his fierce struggles against himself, and towards holiness. It was like hearing Hurrell's voice again, but now uttering more than he had ever done in life. Then Archdeacon Froude asked Newman and other friends to choose themselves a book as a keepsake. Newman had meant to choose a certain book but he found it had already been taken. As he hesitated, a friend said, "Take that." Newman picked up the book. It was a Roman Catholic breviary that Hurrell Froude had possessed and used. Newman looked at it, the psalms, the readings from the Scriptures, the solemn prayers of the ancient Church. He would take it in memory of his friend, and he would use it and love it.

Froude, that most gifted man, had died just when the Oxford Movement had most need of him. Newman turned resolutely to the present—to the immense work that still had to be done.

Froude had gone, but the Movement must go on; it must grow and flourish.

9 – Oriel again and St Mary's

1836 was a year of change for the Newmans. Jemima married John Mozley, a pupil of her brother's, at the end of April, and, less than a month afterwards, all the family joy was turned into mourning because Mrs Newman suddenly fell ill and died. After the funeral service, John stayed on in the church, "lost in prayer and memory". His mind ranged over all the years of his mother's care and love, right up to the last year, when she had laid the foundation stone of the church which he was having built at Littlemore, when she had rejoiced with him that this new church was to rise there to the glory of God. If you go to Littlemore church to-day, you can see on the wall a large plaque, "Sacred to the memory of Jemima Newman", and you can imagine her son praying there so often and thinking sometimes of her as he looked at the building's new timbers and stones.

Harriett was not left long at the house at Iffley, rattling about in it all alone, waiting for John to ride out from Oxford to bear her company of an evening. Later in the year she married Tom, John Mozley's brother. John Mozley was a printer up in Derby and Tom was a clergyman who had a parish in Cholderton in Wiltshire. Perhaps it is as well that Mrs Newman did not live to see Harriett's marriage for she did not wholly approve of Tom. He was a harum-scarum young man who, typically, was nearly late for his brother's wedding because he had lent his best trousers the night before, and had to rush out to retrieve them in the morning. In Cholderton he was a success. The parish sorely needed a Tractarian parson, someone who would revive their sense of worship and reverence, for they had grown so careless in their tiny church that they stacked their umbrellas in the font. He changed all that, but with such a cheerful air that no one minded Parson's rebukes. He and Harriett were gay and happy, and once he chased her all round the house and garden until she had to take refuge in the pig-stye and stay there, shaking with exertion and laughter, and wrinkling her neat, fastidious nose.

So now they were all gone, and that was the end of happy family days at Rose Bank. John Henry went back to permanent residence in his bachelor rooms at Oriel, and perhaps it was as well that Mama was not alive to see him go. She had had her worries, about Charles, of course, and about Harriett, who might marry that unsteady Thomas, and also about John, who, she greatly feared, would never marry at all. She longed to see him "settled" and no doubt she thought, as all who knew him well must have thought, that he would make an admirable family man. He fitted in to all his married friends' households, he was kind and considerate, and the joy of all the children he knew. But when Mrs Newman threw out her motherly hints, John only smiled at her, and his blue eyes wore a remote, unfathomable expression. He would never marry; not that he did not value love and family life, not that he thought it wrong for a clergyman to marry—but that he thought it better to live single, to give all his love and labour directly to God. He had talked about this matter to Hurrell Froude, who had known so much about the lives and the ways of the saints, and who had determined to imitate them in this ideal of a single life, lived for God alone.

Newman sighed a little as he shut the door of Rose Bank for the last time. His family had gone away from him of late, in more senses than one. Charles had gone right away, and Frank was now very much out of sympathy with his eldest brother's religious opinions. Frank's own opinions were changing alarmingly. He began as an Evangelical, and then went on, throwing out one belief after another, like a person lightening the cargo in his ship. First he did not believe in Bishops, lastly he did not even believe in the Trinity. Newman had to admit, too, that none of the womenfolk in his family sympathised fully with the aims of the Oxford Movement. Mrs Newman had spent the last years of her life in a growing perplexity.

Oriel was his only home now. He was partly sorry and partly glad. This was his appointed place—had he not, for years now, intended to live and die here, a bachelor, a don, a clergyman within his college walls? He still had the snapdragon for his emblem, and had obliged Mrs Rickards, when she had wanted a "flower riddle" for her album, with some lines in praise of that cheerful flower that is content to bloom amongst the college stones:

> I am rooted in the wall
> Of buttress'd tower or ancient hall;
> Prisoned in an art-wrought bed,
> Cased in mortar, cramped in lead;
> Of a living stock alone
> Brother of the lifeless stone.
>
> Else unpriz'd I have my worth
> On the spot that gives me birth . . .
> Humble I can bear to dwell
> Near the pale recluse's cell.
> And I spread my crimson bloom
> Mingled with the cloister's gloom. . . .

Be it mine the barren stone
To deck with green life not its own,
So to soften and to grace
Of human works the rugged face.
Mine the unseen to display
In the crowded public way,
Where life's busy arts combine
To shut out the Hand Divine,

Ah! no more a scentless flower,
By approving Heaven's high power,
Suddenly my leaves exhale
Fragrance of the Syrian gale.
Ah! 'tis timely comfort given
By the answering breath of Heaven!
May it be! Then well might I
In College cloister live and die.

Now he could give himself utterly and without distraction to the work of the Movement, and his heart glowed within him at the prospect, for all was going well with the Oxford Movement, and there is great satisfaction for a good and clever man when he can use his energy and his talents for the work he feels God has set him to do. Newman said of the years when he was most concerned with the Movement:

It was, in a human point of view, the happiest time of my life. I was truly at home. I had in one of my volumes appropriated to myself the words of Bramhall, "Bees by the instinct of nature, do love their hives and birds their nests." . . . We prospered and spread.

So back to Oriel to read and write and plan and pray. This Oriel room was very much his own, and typical of him. Two windows looked into the Quadrangle, and two into Merton Lane, so that he had quiet, Oxford scenes before his eyes whenever he lifted his eyes from his books. The room was rather shabbily furnished and carpeted and years before, his sister Mary had teased him about his "brown room" in such tones that you feel she would have loved to come and put up new curtains, and make it generally more bright and comfortable. Over his fireplace was a little picture of his mother, and a plain cross (not a proper crucifix with a figure of Christ upon it, for he thought that would be rather Popish). Books and papers littered his table. There were great bookcases full of the handsome Folios that Pusey had bought for him in Germany, and other volumes of the Fathers that his pupils had given him as a present. There was always a towel in the room, which was there to be used as a duster—not for the furniture, of course, but to dust Newman's precious books. He loved his library so much that sometimes, when he was praying, he asked himself whether he was prepared to part from it if that should be God's will; with equal sincerity he would offer all his books to God, and pray that He would let him keep them.

Leading off his study there was a funny segment of a room; an odd-shaped closet. It lay between Newman's room and the chapel. When he first went in there, he was accosted by an ancient, fishy smell. Whately had those rooms before Newman, and he had used this closet as a larder. He had kept herrings there, hanging on a string. He used to cut a few off for his breakfast and broil them on his fire. One of them had been left there, and Newman found it mouldering on its string, a nasty legacy from Whately. He cleaned out the old fish and the smell with care, because he wanted the little place as an oratory. He hung up a picture of all the saints praying in Heaven. He would go into the oratory, straight from all the work and turmoil of his life, and his heart would lift at the sight of that perpetual adoration. "Why! There you all are—still at it!" he would say, smiling, and then settle to his own prayer. Sometimes he would speak aloud, and Tom Mozley maintained (but you could never trust Tom's stories) that occasionally when you stood in Oriel Quad in the night-time, you could hear the murmur of Newman's voice.

Newman had said his prayers and sharpened his quill, and rummaged for the books he needed. Also, he had "sported his oak". Now he was going to write a sermon to be preached at St Mary's the next day.

And it seemed to him, as he bent to the task, that those old friends spoke to him again, as they used to speak to him when he was a very young Oriel man.

Whately said, "Speak out! Don't be afraid to say what you have to say."

And Hawkins said, "It is not enough to speak out. You must speak clearly. Take pains to choose your words well."

So Newman toiled on, chiselling at his writing, because it was of the utmost importance that his congregation should listen and understand. He was not composing just to inform people, for he was a minister of God, charged with the care of souls, preaching the word of God, and he must strive to reach their very hearts with that message.

In the afternoon of the next day, Sunday, he went across the short distance between Oriel and St Mary's to read the service and to preach. The pews were full, not just with the shopkeepers, who were the real parishioners, but with undergraduates and with other people too. The undergraduates wore a slightly self-righteous air, because they would eat their dinner cold to-day, or miss it altogether—and all because they were going to church. In many colleges the authorities thought that the Tractarians were wrongheaded men with dangerous notions and the Dean in each case, the Fellow who was responsible for discipline, had moved the dinner hour so that no undergraduate should go to St Mary's to hear Mr Newman. Every Head of a college, every Dean knew that Newman and his preaching were the strongest forces to draw the young men to the Movement. Others had turned up out of curiosity, for Newman's fame was growing steadily, and it was now the thing to go to hear him preach.

When the time came for the sermon there was a slight rustle, and then a hush of expectancy in the pews. St

Mary's is a dark church on a winter afternoon, and the gas lights were turned down on these occasions, because Newman's tired eyes could not endure much light. You had to peer a little to see the great man coming down the aisle with that swift, light step of his.

Now he is in the pulpit, standing very still, beginning to read his sermon in a low voice, so that at first you have to strain your ears to hear; but after a minute you realise that you will hear quite well, for his voice (a poet called it "the most entrancing of voices"), though low, is very clear, and he enunciates every word distinctly.

The ladies are hidden inside their bonnets, and the men have their heads bent in a polite Sunday afternoon gesture. If only you could see their faces and learn from their expressions what they are all thinking! Some people here are probably disappointed. They expected a great orator who would excite them with his rich, loud voice, and his splendid gestures, but this man is too quiet and still for an orator; he does not even move his hands. Some other people are disappointed because they expected to have a really thrilling and daring Tractarian sermon, full of attacks and bold statements calculated to shock. But Newman talks of God, of the reality of the spiritual life, of sin, of repentance—matters we have all heard of since our nursery days.

But some people in St Mary's are moved as they have never been moved before, and in a way they had not expected. This quiet man has a strange power. Gladstone, who heard Newman preach, said, "there was a stamp and a seal upon him". He talked of spiritual things with deep conviction, with a kind of restrained energy, so that he seemed to have a knowledge and experience of such matters far beyond that of ordinary men. You might even begin to think that there was something unearthly about him, as you peered through the dimness of the church to see him and hear his silver voice uttering such penetrating wisdom about the world to come. Yet he could talk, too, about temptation and the ordinary life of men with the same penetrating knowledge, so that you knew that he must be a very human person as well as a holy one.

He had a strange way, when he was preaching, of uttering a sentence rather quickly, and then pausing for a minute before he went on. If you go into a monastery church and hear the monks singing their Office, you will hear them singing the psalms in just such a way. They sing half a verse and then pause—utter the words of God, and then wait in quiet and reflection. And prayer and thought are deeper for this alternating of utterance and silence. So it was in Newman's sermons; he spoke and then waited, as if to gather strength, and his listeners could think of his words in the silence.

Someone said of St Mary's and of Newman's preaching there: "Through the stillness of that high Gothic building the words fell like the measured drippings of water in some vast, dim cave." The sentences were indeed like running water, cool and transparent, flowing on, pellucid as a clear stream. Newman could write the most lovely English.

He preached by his words, by his strangely compelling voice, by his own personality, his goodness and sincerity. A great many people who went out from St Mary's on a Sunday afternoon did change their lives from that time. Some of them became Tractarians; some of them did not. But whether or not you joined the Oxford Movement, "you would be harder than most men if you did not feel more than ever ashamed of coarseness, selfishness, worldliness—if you did not feel the things of faith brought closer to the soul".

Newman seemed to talk straight to you, to you personally, to have known exactly what you most needed to hear. He spoke from his heart, directly to your heart.

It was no wonder that he was such a great leader in the Oxford Movement, that his converts and followers revered him deeply, and his enemies feared his power. No wonder that his reputation grew, so that undergraduates would

"When they saw his tall, thin figure going down the High"

turn and stare when they saw his tall, thin figure going down the High, nudge some ignorant freshman and say, "There's Newman!"

10 — Trouble Everywhere

Of course the Tractarians did not have it all their own way. They did not expect to, for they were engaged in holy warfare, and if you go into battle you expect someone to hit at you.

One charge that was levelled at them by all their foes, and even by some of their well-wishers, was that all this harking back to the past, this reviving of ancient Catholic beliefs and customs was extremely dangerous and wrong, because, as sure as a Tractarian was not a Liberal, IT WOULD LEAD TO ROME. This was a severe criticism because, in England a century ago, most people disliked the Church of Rome quite violently.

Stories got about about Romish practices amongst the Tractarian clergy. In fact, there were so many funny stories that Newman, not very seriously, told Maria Giberne that she should make a book of them. A person told a person, who told Newman, that he had called on Dr Pusey, and with his own eyes saw him adore a picture of St Mary. Another person, who had it from a lady at Bath who had it from a French master, knew that Newman wore a large cross down the back of his surplice. Yes, he did! The French master had seen him in St Mary's with his own eyes. Truro people told Keble that lights burned in Littlemore Church, night and day. How did they know, down in Truro? "They had it from an Oxford man." He had gone into the church and found lights burning there; another eye-witness.

Other and stranger stories got about, for instance that the Tractarian clergy offered up sacrifices. "What or whom did they sacrifice? Little children? Or each other?" said Newman with a wry smile. Dr Pusey, travelling in a public coach, heard one lady telling another that Dr Pusey sacrificed a lamb every Friday. He remonstrated gently, but she remained firm in her statement; "she had it on very good authority". "But, madam," he said, in polite anguish, "I am Dr Pusey, and I can assure you that I do not know how to kill a lamb." (Imagine Pusey stabbing lambs; you might as well think of Newman as a likely professional pig-sticker.)

Newman was not really worried by these prophecies, that they would all go over to Rome. Certainly he was less bitter about the Roman Catholic Church than he was in his early days; Froude had taught him to have more respect for that venerable institution. But he had no more intention of becoming a Catholic than he had of becoming a Hindu. He was sure that the Anglican position was right and the Catholic position wrong.

He explained matters like this. There were three roads; one in the middle leading directly to the truth, one on the left and one on the right, both veering away from the truth in opposite directions. One slanting road was the strict Protestant road, and the other was the Roman Catholic road. The true, Church of England road was in the middle. It was a middle way between the two errors, a *Via Media*.

You might put it a different way. Roman Catholics had spoiled the truth that Our Lord had given by adding all sorts of extra beliefs and superstitions that were not there in the days of the early Church. Then the Reformers in the sixteenth century had cast away not only the extra false things, but a great deal that was good. If only the people in the Church of England would take these truths back again and become more like the early Church, they would be exactly right; the Protestants, however, would have too little and the Roman Catholics too much. The picture is rather like that of the man who bought the right shirt; in the advertisement he sits in the middle in a well-fitting shirt, but his companions' shirts have either shrunk or stretched.

The more clearly Newman formulated his ideas, the more the Oxford Movement spread, the greater grew the antagonism of the Liberals. One, called Dr Hampden, was appointed to the important position of Regius Professor of Divinity in the University, and many people, Tractarians and others, opposed the appointment because of Hampden's ideas. The person who suffered most from this affair, however, was Newman because he was pointed at as a cruel persecutor of poor Hampden, though in fact he had always treated Hampden with scrupulous fairness.

Some trouble came to Newman, not from his foes but from his friends. Some of them, particularly the young ones, were excitable, and it was very vexing when he was preaching moderation and saying that Tractarians had no intention of doing rash and Romish things, to have his followers give the lie by what they did and said.

There was Morris of Exeter College for instance, who "did duty" for Newman at St Mary's one Sunday. He chose to preach on the subject of fasting, which was not a popular subject with any but the most fervent Tractarians, and then he added to the offence by saying that animals should fast as well as humans. Newman said that he hoped Morris would get a fasting horse the next time he went steeplechasing!

Another enthusiast who would not smooth the path of public relations was a man called William George Ward. He brought zeal and intelligence to the Oxford Movement, and he also brought trouble. He was a very fat man with a great moon face, whose main interests were philosophy, religion and singing. He used to sing whole operas in his Balliol room, with a friend accompanying on the piano. The quieter Balliol dons must have uttered some ungentlemanly curses when they heard that rich, fat voice uplifted yet again; sometimes a servant was sent round to ask what

Mr Ward was doing. Ward had been a Liberal, but someone had urged him to attend Newman's lectures, and they converted him to a Tractarian way of thinking. These lectures were given in a section of St Mary's called Adam de Brome's chapel. Ward was greatly impressed, and he showed it by making strange faces, by whispering loudly to the friend who had brought him, and by rolling about on the bench like a great beach-ball. Even Newman, who was well-wrapped up in what he was saying, suffered severe distractions, so he asked the verger to change the benches in the chapel so that they would be placed like choir stalls, and the lecturer would not have Ward and his antics directly in front of him.

Ward, once converted, gave out a new creed—"I believe in Newman: Credo in Newmannum." To shout this out, in just those words, was calculated to annoy Newman's enemies, and to annoy Newman too.

However much trouble came, from whatever source, Newman did not worry. He was confident in all he was doing because he believed he was doing what was right; attacks from outside did not matter since he was sure of himself and his cause. Perhaps the early sunshine time of the Movement would not last. Newman had thought of that, even when he was feeling contented like a bee in its hive, or a bird in its nest. But it had not occurred to him that a cloud would come over the sun because he would begin to have doubts himself.

It began with his old friends, the Fathers of the Church. He was busy with lectures, with writing *Tracts for the Times*, and articles for a paper called *The British Critic*. There had been a great many visitors to Oxford that summer, and the leaders of the Movement had been in the public eye more than ever. Newman was glad to settle down in the Long Vacation to his beloved Fathers again. One night he took down one of his precious tomes to read again the history of how St Leo fought some heretics called the Monophysites—and he was appalled to find that the story did not read to him as it used to do. The attitude of the heretics seemed dreadfully like the attitude of the Anglicans. St Leo, his friend, seemed to look at him sternly. Was it possible that the Roman Catholics were the true friends, the true spiritual descendants of St Leo, and that he, Newman, was backing up a heresy against the Church of God? How horrible to look into a mirror and find that you were not the person that you expected. . . . Newman looked into the mirror of history and saw his own times reflected in the fifth century, and when he looked at his own face he found himself a Monophysite.

Perhaps it was all a mistake. The idea came, and it went. And then it came again in a different form. Newman did not have it straight out of his own head this time, but thrust at him by an old acquaintance, Monsignor Wiseman. Ever since Wiseman had met Newman and Froude in Rome he had been interested in the Tractarians, and he thought that, given some time and some pushing, they would become Roman Catholics. So he busied himself writing articles calculated to show them the error of their ways. One article in the *Dublin Review* was brought to Newman's notice, and he was struck most forcibly by one passage. Wiseman quoted St Augustine giving judgment against some more heretics, the Donatists, and again Newman felt that the Donatists stood then much as the Tractarians were to do centuries later. St Augustine was not his friend. Things were worse than that, because he knew that St Augustine was speaking the truth that the Church in his day had received from the Apostles. And they had received it from Christ our Lord.

St Augustine thundered against the Donatists, in Latin, saying that they were speaking for a little part of the world, but only the whole of the Catholic world could judge with confidence. "*Securus iudicat orbis terrarum . . .*" The stately syllables sounded again and again in Newman's ears. They sounded as "Turn again Whittington" sounded for Dick Whittington in the chime of the bells. He could not forget them for a time. Perhaps he, Newman, was quite in the wrong. Perhaps he and the other Tractarians were not working in the cause of right and truth. The idea gave him a stomach-ache. He thought the Tractarian ship had sprung a leak.

In the October of that year, 1839, he went walking in the New Forest with an Oxford friend, Henry Wilberforce, and he told him something of what was on his mind. Newman looked soberly at the long lines of trees in their autumnal bronze and gold, and said, "A vista has opened before me, to the end of which I do not see."

His friend knew that he was not referring to the trees. Was the end of the vista—Rome? It was too distant and too dreadful to be spoken of plainly. Wilberforce said in a low voice, "I would rather you died than you should take such a step." He felt cold, and he noticed that the leaves were beginning to drift down. The fall of the year suddenly seemed a very melancholy thing. If Newman were to leave them, the Spring would go out of their year for ever.

But Newman would not leave them yet. Again the idea came, and it went. The sky opened and it closed again. Newman continued much as before, believing much as he used to believe. But, as he said himself, a man who has seen a ghost is not afterwards as if he had never seen it. His confidence was shaken.

In Lent, 1840, he decided to go up to Littlemore, away from the arguments in Oxford, to pray and fast and preach and serve his people. He stayed in lodgings, in Mrs Barnes' house, and he kept Lent properly. He took no meat, except a little cold bacon, no fish, butter, vegetables, fruit, pastry, sugar, tea, wine, beer or toast. On Wednesdays and Fridays he did not have anything to eat or drink at all until supper-time, and then he had two eggs, some bread and some barleywater. He wrote in his Journal in a rather self-accusing way, that he had not slept on the ground, nor had he tried to cut short his sleep. But since he was usually up until midnight and always rose very early, he does not appear to have been very lazy.

What Mrs Barnes thought, goodness knows. The only

time she was able to try to cosset her reverend lodger was when he got a horrible cold. She served him with some hot concoction, "some precious mess", and put it on the fender to keep hot until he went to bed, and she assured him that if he took it faithfully for three nights (like a magic potion) he could not tell the deal of good it would do him. So then, no doubt, Mrs Barnes felt better for having administered the remedy, and there was another penance provided for Newman.

He visited his parishioners, the old, the sick, the people who were troubled in their minds, the black sheep.

Then he got to work on the school-children. They did not look very hopeful, he thought, when they were all arrayed before him, especially the girls. The schoolmistress was no good, and consequently all the little girls were scruffy, with dirty hands and faces and rough hair. When they did sewing, that was grimy too. Also they were ignorant; the top girls hardly knew Adam from Noah. Newman was perplexed for, as he said, "he was not deep in the philosophy of schoolgirl tidiness". But he dealt with the situation manfully, told them all to tidy themselves, set them to knitting stockings and gave them white pinafores as presents, to wear in church.

Another problem was that of punctuality. The children did not turn up in time for catechism. He wrote anxiously to Jemima to say that he did not know what to do, short of going round and visiting the parents. Should he bribe the children?

Gradually he worked his reform. The girls became clean and tidy, and both boys and girls began to take an interest in their catechism, and answered up very brightly. Newman strung up his fiddle and led them in singing "Gregorians" in the schoolroom.

Up in his room at Mrs Barnes' Newman sat and blew his nose and the Lenten cold struck into him. He held his pen in stiff fingers (his hands were getting red and rough because he had given up his gloves for Lent) and he wrote for himself an account of his earlier journeyings in Sicily. He ended with the story of Gennaro who had wanted New-man's cloak ("cloke" as Newman always wrote it, in the old-fashioned spelling) as a recompense for his services. That blue cloak was still with him. He had it on his bed up here at Littlemore when nights were cold. It was a very old friend by now. Then with a smile at his own touch of self-pity he wrote, "I have so few things to sym-pathize with me that I take to clokes."

Then he went to bed, blew out his candle, tucked his cold feet under the "cloke" and went to sleep very peace-fully. He was overworked, he had a cold, he was fasting, chilly and lonely. But he was doing the Lord's work, and he was a great deal happier in Littlemore than he would have been dining and wining and talking down in Oriel.

Then Easter came, and they had a very happy festival in Littlemore church. The children were there, spruce and interested and singing like anything. The villagers had brought flowers for the chancel, roses and sweetbriar, so that the church smelt like the Holy Sepulchre. Newman was very much at peace.

Then he went down into Oxford again, down into his beloved city that looked so beautiful and so welcoming when he looked at its glittering spires in the valley. There he would soon meet the biggest trouble he had ever known.

11 — *The College at Littlemore*

Newman had just one more year's residence at Oxford, though he did not know this at the time. Already he was turning over in his mind what he would say in the next Tract he was going to write and, when this Tract did come out in February 1841, it exploded like a bomb and New-man went out of Oxford with the blast. This was Tract 90, the last and most famous of the *Tracts for the Times.*

This Tract was all about the Thirty-nine Articles. They are statements of Church of England belief, drawn up in the sixteenth century, and set out in the Book of Common Prayer. Every clergyman has to sign a declaration that he holds by what they state and, at this time, so did every member of the University of Oxford. The Articles seemed to be of a strictly Protestant mind, and the signing of them might be a trouble to a Tractarian conscience. Newman felt he really must explain the matter or else some Tractarians would begin to think that the Church of England officially held by strictly Protestant beliefs. It would be disastrous if anyone were to think this; it would be an encouragement to go over to Rome. Newman was quite sure himself that the Thirty-nine Articles could, in all straightforwardness and truth, be interpreted according to Tractarian ideas. Their Protestant look was the result of the historical circumstances in which they were written. Of course, just after the Reformation, Articles drawn up by the Church of England would deny the errors and superstitions of Rome, in no uncertain terms, but this did not mean a rejection of true Catholic belief. This Protestant appearance that the Articles had was a dusty covering that obscured the truth; Newman had only to rub with his duster and the truth would shine out brightly. Newman did not expect that everyone would accept his interpretation, but it was a perfectly honest and possible interpretation and he sent the pamphlet to the publishers with an untroubled mind.

When Tract 90 appeared, however, there was a dreadful commotion. The Anti-Tractarians howled with rage. The cry was raised that Newman was leading the Church of England to Popery. The Heads of the Houses in Oxford were loud against it too, and the Bishop, alarmed, told Newman that this dangerous Tract must be the last of the series. The great men of Oxford did not act quite independently, as Newman realised, for they were stirred up by a strange man named Golightly. He had been a Tractarian and now he was an avowed enemy, and he dearly liked to collect gossip so that he could go round making trouble with it. He had a most exciting time posting copies of Tract 90 to Bishops, and going round to the Heads of the Colleges to talk and be made much of. "Golly" became a "Great Man". He was a little unbalanced; he used to look about shiftily and say he was nervous about going home in the dark in case the Tractarians set about him. It was not really likely to any sane observer that Newman would lurk in Oxford lanes to beat up his enemies with cudgels.

Oxford, and indeed England at large, were against Tract 90 and its author, and were so violent and vehement that

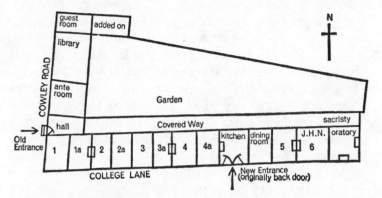

he was surprised. He looked very rueful and said, "I fear we are clean dished!"

This commotion strengthened a resolve Newman was making at this time—to leave Oxford with its clamour and give himself to a quiet life of prayer and study. He was no longer sure that he was doing what was right, no longer convinced of the Church of England's title to be called part of the Catholic Church. He was in a growing darkness and he wanted to seek the light of God in prayer and thought and penance.

Littlemore was his place of refuge, and he looked about there for somewhere more suitable for his purpose than lodgings with Mrs Barnes. There was for sale a block of stables, near Littlemore Church, and Newman thought it would do very well. He did not intend to live alone all of the time; he would offer his strange new home as a refuge for any Tractarian men who also wanted a quiet place. These stables, built like an "L" would divide up into sets of little rooms. He had the builders in when he had completed his purchase, and eventually the "College" was arranged to his liking. Now it has been restored and we know exactly what it was like in Newman's day, as you can see from the diagram on p. 89.

It was a poor little place, more like the parish workhouse in appearance than anything else. There were cold brick floors, a very low roof, small windows. A low verandah or shed ran the whole length of the buildings, and to get from one part to another, you had to use this rough passage-way and meet a gust of fresh air there, since one side was open to the garden. The large barn was fitted out with shelves to hold Newman's library, and he bought a stove to heat this important room. It was a temperamental stove, and Newman had some long and dusty wrestlings with it. Inmates turned up, as he had thought they would: young men, John Dalgairns, Frederick Bowles, William Lockhart, Richard Stanton, and a particularly pleasant young man called Ambrose St John. A sort of little community began to grow up, though no one was a permanent fixture except Newman himself.

Life there was hard and strict. They rose early and spent many hours praying in the church and also in the little room in the house they had set apart as an oratory. It had no window and was hung around with red stuff. In Lent the Littlemore community had a retreat (as well as a daunting fast) and meditated there, an hour at a time. It was stuffy and crowded in that little, square, airless room, and Newman would surface after some spell of deep thought and prayer, shuffle a little and sigh, and wonder when the hour would end. Meals were plain and not very frequent. Breakfast was taken in the Spartan refectory at a kind of sideboard (known rudely as the "pig-trough"), and it was eaten standing in silence.

Yet it was happy there. The prayer of Littlemore, the

voluntary poverty brought them nearer to Our Lord, and so hearts were tranquil and spirits gay. Newman created a genuine family life there, and they had the unity and the kind feelings, the jokes that a good family has. After dinner they would gather in the Library for the intelligent, lively talk that Newman could stimulate. He would not have church gossip or pious chatter. The fiddle would come out of its green baize bag and he would play, and someone would unlock the little closet where the treats were kept (wine, tea and jam) and set the tea-kettle boiling. Newman always had the tea flowing freely. The garden bloomed under St John's skilful fingers for he was a keen gardener. Bowles dug up some bulbs from his mother's garden when at home and brought them back to plant at Littlemore.

You would think that Newman would have been left in peace in his house and garden, but he was not. Angry rumours flew about that a Popish monastery was being established up at Littlemore, and nosey parkers came down from Oxford to pry into Newman's building. "I cannot walk into or out of my house but curious eyes are upon me," he said, and told of a shameful incident.

One day, when I entered my house, I found a flight of undergraduates inside. Heads of Houses, as mounted patrols walked their horses round those poor cottages. Doctors of Divinity dived into the hidden recesses of that private tenement and drew domestic conclusions from what they saw there. I had thought that an Englishman's house was his castle. . . .

And the nosey parkers for the newspapers wanted to know why he went up to Littlemore. He did not want to tell them that he went up there to say his prayers, nor did he want to tell the world that he had a doubt of the Anglican system. If he did not tell his most private thoughts to the world he was thought to be dishonest, and if, as he did on other occasions, he gave out his reasons and motives, people said his real reasons were different from the ones he gave. Whatever he did or said, whatever he did not say,

Newman was known for a very sly fellow. This is a very strange judgment, for Newman was a singularly honest person. He did not tell lies, not even to himself. Perhaps if you are as honest as that, the world cannot believe that you are as you seem.

Newman was not afraid of those jealous, prying eyes, but he had a fear in his heart, up at Littlemore; he was afraid lest he should offend God. More and more he was unhappy about the Church of England. As time went on, attacks had multiplied against Tract 90, and they came from the Bishops. Also there were other signs that the Bishops believed the Church to be a strictly Protestant institution. Now this was really serious. Newman believed in obedience to the Bishops and here they were denying beliefs that he held to be fundamental to the Christian Faith. To add to his doubts, his private "ghost" had come again, the ghost of the past. The Arian heretics rose up against him this time, when he was busy writing about St Athanasius, heretics who grinned and gibbered and claimed him as one of themselves.

His heart was wrung. If only his decisions were just for himself! But he had long been so important in the Oxford Movement, so much a trusted guide for people's souls that whatever he did would affect many others. This thought weighed unbearably on his conscience. Suppose that he announced that he now doubted what he had earlier proclaimed to be true, and so provoked his followers to doubt, would they not lose all confidence and faith and perhaps doubt Christianity altogether? And suppose, after all, his doubts were ill-founded?

Was there anyone to help him? Pusey could not. Keble could not, though he tried to advise his friend. Pusey and Keble never had any doubts of the Church of England, so there was nothing they could do for Newman.

Just now Newman could have done with a word of sympathy from his family. But he did not get it. When things were very bad, news came that Charlie had come home from Germany (where he had been in prison for not paying his rent) and money was needed to set him up yet again. Frank at this juncture was good at supplying money to help with Charlie, but he was not helpful to John in his religious doubts. He told him to go off and start his own religion—he'd find that a satisfactory solution! His eldest brother was stunned. Did truth not matter at all to Frank?

There was a great row with Harriett too. Tom was the cause of it because on holiday in France he became very attracted to the Church of Rome, and came home ahead of his wife, highly excited and ready to talk about the matter with his brother-in-law. Newman did not like fast, excited conversions, and he always restrained the men at Littlemore when they had an attack of Roman fever. He went down to Cholderton and calmed Tom satisfactorily. Then Harriett came home and heard all about the incident. Little, bossy Harriett was annoyed with Tom, and she made up her mind that never again would he begin to stray from the Anglican path. He never did. She was still more annoyed with her luckless brother. That was what came of all this near-Popish thought of his. She never forgave John for this.

Jemima, a kinder, more gentle person, was the only one left to him. She wrote to her brother and even visited him once at Littlemore, bringing her eldest son with her (the little boy's name was Herbert, a sad disappointment to his Uncle John who had so hoped, when he was born on St Athanasius' day, that the child would be called Athanasius Mozley); but Jemima could not understand very much of what her brother was thinking and feeling, and she met his long and honest letters with disheartening silences. The silences grew and the sympathy diminished, and Jemima, too, became a stranger.

At last Newman came to the point when he felt he must resign from his living of St Mary's and Littlemore. On Sunday, 24th September, 1843, he preached his last sermon in the Church of England. It was the anniversary of the Littlemore church's consecration. Dr Pusey came to take the service, and many of Newman's friends came to rejoice in the little church's festival and to sorrow at this parting. The villagers were there, loyal and puzzled that their beloved Parson should be resigning. The children were there, the little girls smart again in new pinafores and bonnets that were Newman's present. Again the church was bright with flowers, not the sweetbriar of Eastertime now, but dahlias and other flowers with the rich and heady colours of autumn.

Newman urged them, as he did at all times, to "do that which is good" and then he bade them farewell.

And O my brethren, O kind and affectionate hearts, O loving friends, should you know anyone whose lot it has been, by writing or by word of mouth, in some degree to help you thus to act; if he has ever told you what you knew about yourselves or what you did not know; has ever read to you your wants or feelings, and has comforted you by the very reading; has made you feel that there was a higher life than this daily one, and a brighter world than that you see; or encouraged you, or sobered you, or opened a way to the enquiring, or soothed the perplexed, if what he has said or done has ever made you take an interest in him, and feel well-inclined towards him, remember such a one in time to come, though you hear him not, and pray for him that in all the things he may know God's will, and at all times he may be ready to fulfil it.

Newman's sermons were often moving. This one was almost overpowering. It was no disgrace in those days to weep in public, even if you were a grown man; rather, it was strange not to show your feelings. On this occasion Pusey and everyone else in the packed church were in tears.

When he had finished Newman took off his gown and hood and threw them over the communion rail. The little gesture had a dreadful air of finality.

The Littlemore villagers had not seen the last of him, although he had resigned his living. It was in fact two

94

more years before Newman left the Church of England altogether. Why did he linger so long? He said himself, "I was on my deathbed as regards my membership with the Anglican Church" from the end of 1841, and indeed he was an unconscionable time a-dying. Unkind things were said both by Anglicans and Catholics. Some Anglicans believed that Newman was already a secret Catholic, probably a Jesuit, paid to stay on at Littlemore to lure men into the Roman spider's web; some Catholics muttered meanly that he lingered in the Church of England through fear or self-interest.

He stayed, in fact, because he had no choice. He could not be a Catholic until his conscience told him that he ought to be. He had to be sure. Meanwhile he prayed, sifted his motives, bore the burden of doubt, and began to write a book called *The Development of Christian Doctrine*. There he examined an idea that he was deeply interested in, and tried to see how the truth that Our Lord taught us is at once fixed and unchanging as rock and yet capable of growth like a living tree.

One Catholic did help him in his anxious seeking time, an Irish priest called Dr Russell. He was always quiet and patient; he did not hint, or nag or cajole, or talk religion, or stir up argument. He did not treat Newman like a winkle to be teased out by a Catholic pin.

Another sadness came now, two deaths that were so good and resigned that Newman had additional proofs of something he already knew well, and never would deny, that there were people living and dying in the Church of England in great holiness. One who died was Lucy Pusey, Dr Pusey's daughter, at the age of fifteen. When she was a small child she played with Newman, wore his spectacles for a joke, listened to his fairy stories. Later she heard his sermons, and read them over again in a book, using them as a guide for her life. You can still see the volume of sermons with "Lucy Pusey" written on the flyleaf in her careful child's handwriting. It is moving to see it, to handle a book that helped her to live so well that she could die at fifteen, joyous and smiling in spite of pain, quite ready to end her life so early since it was God's will. Newman said she was a saint.

The other was Newman's old friend, handsome, pleasant John William Bowden. He died of the dreaded consumption, leaving his wife and four children. Newman visited him in his last and lingering illness and saw Bowden quite patient, as cheerful and affectionate as ever. He had to be carried up to bed by two servants, and instead of resenting his helplessness, he joked about his "procession" as he was carried up, with his wife going ahead with the candle. When Bowden died Newman said :

> I sobbed bitterly over his coffin to think that he had left me still dark as to what the way of truth was, and what I ought to do to please God and fulfil His will.

Griefs within, attacks without. In a cold, bleak February (1845) news came that a major attack was to be launched on the Tractarians. W. G. Ward, the enthusiastic fat man, had written a very Popish book called *The Ideal of a Christian Church*. The senior members of the University were to gather together, in Convocation, to pass censure on Ward and take his degree away from him. They decided, at the last minute, to condemn Newman's Tract 90 at the same time. This was a mean action, for Tract 90 was long out of print. It was like digging up a dead enemy and hanging his skeleton.

It had been snowing hard when Convocation met in the Sheldonian. Ward rolled along, very cheerful, with notes of his speech in his fat, capable fist. He did not really care what the University did to him. He slipped and fell in the snow, scattering his papers, and the undergraduates, crowding outside, cheered like mad.

"Good old Ward," said one undergraduate, squeezing up a handful of snow to make another missile. "Did you know he is engaged to be married?"

"No!" said another, delighted and laughing. Ward had been saying for some time how much he reverenced the single life. "Never mind, Ward, though. Here comes the Vice-Chancellor!"

And as he came, with his attendants, in stately procession, the undergraduates let fly with their snowballs, whizz and slosh. Some of them just did it for fun. Some of them thought, rightly, that the Vice-Chancellor and his friends had behaved meanly.

Ward and his book were condemned. Newman's Tract 90 was in fact spared, but only because the Proctors, who were Newman's friends, had a right to veto, and used it. When the proposed condemnation was read out, a loud Latin shout from these two stopped the proceedings.

"Non placet! Non placet!"

But everyone knew that, in the eyes of most of the University, Newman stood condemned.

12 — *Father Dominic comes to Littlemore*

It was becoming clear that it was time for Newman to move. Some of his younger friends could not bear to wait any longer, and hopped off from Littlemore, sending word later that they had been received into the Church of Rome. The news of each conversion was received with dismay in Anglican circles. "He has gone!" they would say. "I am afraid So-and-so has GONE." Gone, vanished, stepped off into space, or so you would think from their dismal phrasing.

Newman, meanwhile, was drawing near the end of his book. It had done a great deal of work in its author for, before he had finished, he saw clearly in his mind yet another picture of the Church, as of a great tree, the same for ever, and rooted in unchanging truth, but living and growing and spreading its branches further. It no longer worried him that the Roman Church had devotions and teachings that were not found in the same form in the early Church. They were not new doctrines, made by man, but had grown from the beginning, as a daffodil grows from a bulb, or an oak from an acorn, or as a great tree grows from a mustard seed. Newman laid down his pen. It was time for him to seek admission into the Roman Catholic Church.

It was, in a human way, like stepping into chilly waters. Most converts have some Catholic relative or friend, or they have become familiar with Catholic services, and they know a church or two; they have some warm human comforts to look forward to in their new life. Newman had very little in the way of Catholic contacts. He who valued friends and warm, familiar homely things, had to go with little to help him on except the knowledge that he was following his conscience. He did not go quite alone, though, because his greatest friend of the Littlemore community became a Catholic just before he did. This was Ambrose St John, the friend that God gave Newman when He took everything else away.

It was obvious to the outside world that the end was in sight. So the gossips were busy, the great were curious. Dr Wiseman was now a Bishop in England, at the new Catholic college of Oscott near Birmingham. He sent a new convert, Bernard Smith, over to Littlemore to see how Newman was getting on. Smith came back looking very knowing.

"What did he say?" said Wiseman eagerly.

"Nothing," said young Smith. "But he won't be long now."

"How do you know?"

"I know from his trousers."

"His TROUSERS?"

"Yes. He was wearing grey trousers for dinner, and if he has left off his black clericals it must mean he thinks he is a layman really."

Now Newman thought no such thing, and he did not

98

buy a special pair of trousers in order to tip the wink to the Oscott spy, but still Bernard Smith would have his little story.

Newman did manage to keep his going quiet. So personal a matter should not be an occasion for public stir and fuss. He cut the last link that bound him and resigned his Oriel Fellowship. Now he had to find a priest to receive him into the Roman Catholic Church. This problem solved itself, for news came that an Italian priest, Father Dominic Barberi, who had received Dalgairns into the Church, was calling to see his new convert as he was on his way to Belgium. Newman had met Father Dominic before, and reverenced him as a holy man. He later described the start of the Italian priest's life like this:

> On the Apennines, near Viterbo, there dwelt a shepherd boy in the first years of this century, whose mind had early been drawn heavenward, and one day as he prayed before an image of the Madonna, he felt a vivid intimation that he was destined to preach the Gospel under the northern sky. There appeared no means by which a Roman peasant could be turned into a missionary . . . yet though no external means appeared, the inward impression did not fade; on the contrary it became more definite, and in process of time, instead of the dim north, England was engraved on his heart.

"On the Apennines, near Viterbo, there dwelt a shepherd boy . . ." It sounds like the opening of a fairy tale, and indeed, the life of Dominic Barberi has the beauty and strangeness of an old and magic legend. But his story is not of the airy stuff of fantasy; it bears the mark of the wonderful providence of God. He joined the religious congregation of the Passionists when he was young and, since he was poor and unlettered, he was to be a lay-brother. Yet, if he was to fulfil his own strange prediction about himself, he would have to be a priest in order to come to preach in England. Sure enough, his Superiors found out that he was clever, and had him educated for the priesthood. And then, for years and years, he was kept at work in Italy, so that it seemed that his dream would never be fulfilled.

Eventually he was sent—a strange, foreign figure in English eyes. He spoke little English when he first came, and he wore his Passionist habit, a black tunic and cloak, with an emblem of Our Lord's Passion sewn on it, with sandals on his bare feet, so that he looked foreign and popish. Alternatively, he wore black "ordinary" clothes, but since he was a most austere, poor man, he wore what he could pick up, and the net result was amazing. His coat did not fit, and it was wrongly buttoned. His trousers did not fit either, and his waistcoat had obviously belonged to a tramp before he had it. His boots were ancient and patched, and quite without polish, and he wore the most wretched hat in England. He carried on his journeyings a vast watch, and an enormous ancient trunk, to hold anything useful that he might be given, so that he could take it back to the Passionist house he was founding here in England. He might be given some potatoes, or some boots that would do for the gardener, and they all went into the trunk.

England was changing now from the place that Newman had known in his boyhood, when Catholics were few and lived retired. They were still a very small minority, viewed with suspicion, and the old Catholic families lived quietly still and kept themselves to themselves. But in the new industrial cities of the North, and in the Midlands, Irish immigrants were providing a new Catholic section of the population. Father Dominic found more than enough to do, as he toiled up and down England, using the railway for the long distances and his own weary feet for the shorter ones. He preached missions, heard confessions, received converts. He poured out his labour and his love, and very often he was laughed at and pelted with mud.

It was this man who was coming for a brief stay at Littlemore, on 8th October 1845. It was a wild, rainy day, and Dalgairns was going to meet Father Dominic off the coach, which would reach Oxford at ten o'clock that night.

He went to get his hat and walking stick. Newman met him and said in a low voice, "When you see your friend, will you tell him that I wish him to receive me into the Church of Christ?"

Dalgairns set off, and in a short while Ambrose St John joined him. It did not seem a time for discussion, and they went in silence over the squelchy fields, praising God in their hearts. At the "Angel" inn, Oxford, the coach came in. Father Dominic had travelled on top because that was cheaper, though wetter, than going inside, and as he was in the very act of dismounting, Dalgairns broke the news to him. "God be praised!" said Father Dominic, and they said no more all the way back to Littlemore, going in a chaise that Dalgairns had ordered to pick them up at the inn. Father Dominic was soaked. Little rivulets ran off him, and his cracked boots were waterlogged.

When they got home, they showed him straightaway into Newman's own room, where a fire was crackling in the grate. He sat down and looked around the little bare room, and he marvelled that a man who could have had the comfort of an Oxford life for as long as he wished should have chosen to live here, as poor as a monk. Father Dominic was a short man, but he could put up his hand and touch the ceiling when he stepped inside the Littlemore front door. The only comfortable thing in this poor room was the fire, and he was uncommonly glad of it. He got as close to the blaze as he could, and began to steam gently. His old clothes gave off the odour of a wet sheepdog.

The door opened and Newman came in, with his characteristic quick, light step. He did not waste time in preliminaries, but fell on his knees in front of Father Dominic and asked him to hear his confession. It seems odd to make one's confession in two instalments, but that is what he did; he did half of it that night, and then, since it was by now very late, they went to bed, Father Dominic in the little guest-house at the other end of the building.

And no one knew or guessed, not Wiseman over in his

episcopal bed at Oscott, or "Golly" Golightly down in Oxford, tossing uneasily in a nightmare of Tractarians rushing upon him, what was happening in the stable-house in Littlemore.

The wind still howled and the rain dripped from the trees and gutters and ran down the small window panes. The little fire fell in with a soft crash of coals and died out in Newman's grate.

In the morning Father Dominic went down into Oxford to the little Catholic church in St Clement's to say his Mass and to make arrangements about borrowing things so that he could offer Mass at Littlemore next day. Newman meanwhile went on with his letters. He had about thirty to do in all, and already a large pile were written and ready for the post; the stack would not go until he was received into the Church. Henry Wilberforce had one, Mrs Bowden, Pusey. Keble, when he got his letter, was afraid to open it, thinking that he knew its contents, and he kept it in his pocket all day. Other Tractarian friends had the news too: a letter for Frederick Faber, another for Henry Manning, Maria Giberne. One for poor old Aunt Betsey who lived with Jemima, and who would be greatly upset. It hurts to write a letter containing news that is a joy to your own heart but will bring only pain to those you love.

He had written to Jemima:

Littlemore. Oct. 8, 1845.

My dear Jemima,

I must tell you, what will pain you greatly, but I will make it as short as you would wish me to do.

This night Father Dominic the Passionist sleeps here. He does not know of my intention, but I shall ask him to receive me into what I believe to be the One Fold of the Redeemer.

This will not go till all is over.

Ever Yours affectly,
JOHN H. NEWMAN.

When they were done, his hand ached unbearably. He felt very tired altogether, and in between whiles he went and lay down on his bed.

In the evening he finished his confession. Bowles and Stanton went to confession too, and Father Dominic received all three of them into the Church. The next morning, the 10th, Mass was said in the little oratory, on a makeshift altar erected on Henry Wilberforce's little writing desk, and Newman made his First Communion.

The next day, a Saturday, Father Dominic said Mass again for them, and then set off for Belgium. He and Newman parted with mutual affection and respect. Father Dominic said that Newman was one of the most humble and lovable men he had ever met.

Then on Sunday they could not have Mass in their own house (indeed Mass was not said again in the Littlemore Oratory until a hundred years later), so they walked into Oxford to St Clement's, and people watching could guess why Mr Newman and his friends were walking St Clement'swards on a Sunday morning. ("Ah, so poor Newman has gone over at last.")

Father Dominic had gone to continue his work for God and the Church, travelling from mission to mission via the railways that were changing the face of England. He wore himself out and not many years later fell mortally ill in a train and was taken to the Railway Hotel at Reading, where he died.

Newman, aged forty-four, had felt so tired and unwell this last year or so that he thought he probably would not have a long life. But whatever time he had he would spend it working for God and the Church too, though in his own way, not Father Dominic's. He would give all his talents and his energies, just as he had done for the Oxford Movement.

Had he been able to look into the future, he might have been daunted. He did work for the Catholic Church in England, with all his strength, and in nearly every project he was thwarted. It was, in some ways, a dreary future that lay before him, and it was a much longer one than he thought. He was to live to be eighty-nine, so he was, in fact, just half-way through.

13 — Oscott and Maryvale

At the end of the month Newman went to Oscott, the big, new, Gothic-style Catholic college housing schoolboys and older seminary students, where Bishop Wiseman, Newman's new source of authority, had his headquarters. It was an embarrassing meeting. They sat in a parlour, Wiseman asking stilted questions about the journey there, and Newman, in a shy fit, making short, polite answers that crashed like stones in a chilly pool. An awful silence fell. Wiseman looked about for some means of escape, and was glad when a message was brought in that one of the boys wanted to go to confession. "O, certainly" said the Bishop. "You will excuse me, Mr Newman?" And forth he rushed, causing the boy to wonder at his speed and affability.

The next day, the feast of All Saints, Newman was confirmed in the Oscott chapel. He had to choose a new name, a new heavenly patron, and he chose "Mary". He had a great devotion to Our Lady. So much of his life had been under her protection: Oriel's Foundation Day was the feast of her Purification; Newman's church had been St Mary's, and Littlemore, he felt, was specially under her care. "Nor did she do nothing for me in that lowly habitation," he said in a quiet phrase that at once disclosed and hid some of his meaning.

Then he talked further with Wiseman, and they were friendlier now. What were he and his friends to do, and where were they to go? Wiseman had a house called Old Oscott, where the college had been until the architect

Pugin had built the new one, and he kindly offered it for Newman's use. They could have their community life there, as at Littlemore, until they had decided what to do. Newman accepted the offer and, again thinking of Our Lady, named the house "Maryvale". It is a tall, plain house. Its forbidding front is made more pleasant by its spreading garden, and a large semi-circular loggia with a grapevine, and by a certain rustic air it has, even now, when Birmingham has spread in a rash of little dreary houses right up to Maryvale's wall. Inside it is dark and "dismally ugly", as Newman said, but it was conveniently self-supporting, with its own bakehouse and brewhouse.

There was another visit to Oscott on St Cecilia's Day, and again Newman was unintentionally a source of embarrassment to Bishop Wiseman. He turned up in the evening when the college were having a musical party in honour of the day. As he approached he could hear the familiar, welcome sound of fiddles being tuned. They were taking refreshments in between items, great hunks of cake, and some liquid served in tall jugs. "Just lemonade, you know. Hm-m-m," said Wiseman, escorting his guest to the high table.

Newman was helped to some of it and it made him gasp. It was remarkably stiff punch, and he had to dilute it with twice or thrice its quantity of water. "Lemon and sugar, and just a little drop of . . ." said Wiseman, and then, to his further mortification, he heard those wretched boys striking up a music-hall song. What would the strict-living Mr Newman think? As a matter of fact, he was highly amused.

No wonder Wiseman thought Newman and his friends were almost too strict, and too good to live. Father Dominic, with the best will in the world, had been making things difficult for his new converts. He read with indignation an attack on them in a Catholic paper and hastened to reply. He described their strict and prayerful life at Littlemore (imagine having an account of your penances in the paper) and then, trying his very best with his English, he perpetrated an elaborate series of puns that set everyone laughing.

Those walls bear testimony that the Catholic is a *little more* than the Protestant Church, the soul a *little more* than the body, eternity a *little more* than the present time. Understand well this *little more* and I am sure you will do a *little more* for your eternal salvation.

This report on his own life had to be borne "as one bears a stomach-ache", said Newman, for grumbling would do no good.

Littlemore now had to be abandoned. Ambrose St John went ahead to Maryvale to wrestle with the painters and get the house ready. Newman put his books in crates (they were always his first care) and dealt with all the manifold business of packing and moving. It was a mercy he had long, practical experience of such matters, for his family, in their many moves, had left much of the business to John. In his clearing up he found the usual mixture of important things and junk, first a philosophical manuscript and then a lump of resin and an inkglass. It was sad, picking the Littlemore house to pieces. He was very fond of it, and he was going to a new life so strange and unknown that it felt like going out on the open sea.

He was content to go, not knowing anything about the future. When he said in his poem "Lead, kindly Light" "one step enough for me", he had done much more than express pious sentiments in some neat verses; he had meant every word he said. But faith and trust in God do not take away the pain that the human heart feels. Sacrifice hurts, thought it is offered joyfully.

Every stick and stone of Littlemore seemed to take on a friendly, human semblance (just as the old "cloke" had done) and he could hardly tear himself away. It was foolish, perhaps, but there was no one there to see him, so he kissed the mantelpiece and the bed before he left.

Then he went down into Oxford to make his last farewells, and dined with a friend. Another good friend,

Richard Church, called to see him, and Pusey, and an old tutor from Trinity. In him he wished goodbye to his first college, the college that had been kinder to him than Oriel had ever been. He remembered the snapdragon that grew in Trinity, on the walls, the symbol, as he had thought, of his own "perpetual residence in his University". The next morning he left, and twenty years later he wrote this sad sentence: "I have never seen Oxford since, excepting its spires, as they are seen from the railway."

Now he settled down to life at Maryvale. It was community life as before, and, on the whole, cheerful. Ambrose St John was in charge of the food, and said he could not get on with his studying because his mind was full of roast meat and jam roly. Newman formed a little choir, and was obliged to cast forth St John and some others who were most unmusical and formed the "awkward squad". There is always at least one nuisance in a community, and in this one it was Morris, he who had once preached on fasting animals. His job, he said, would be that of carpenter, and Newman was glad to hear it because there was plenty of work in that line, and there was a lot of shelving to be done in the library. But Morris' idea of being house-carpenter was to fit up his own bookshelves, and when he was wanted for anything else he was not to be found, because he was out, dining over at Oscott.

They looked different now from their Littlemore selves, because they were wearing cassocks and Roman collars (Church of England clergymen did not wear a "dog-collar" in those days). They were not priests yet, but they were to be ordained and Wiseman was to give them Minor Orders at Oscott. Those young men who had previously sported whiskers now had to shave them off. Some of them rather enjoyed their new Roman rig, but Newman felt shy and conspicuous, and scowled at the idea of wearing a biretta.

There were worse inflictions than having to wear a funny hat and a stiff, unfamiliar collar. Wiseman provided trials, though probably without meaning to. The "old Catholics", trained by circumstances to caution, and even to suspicion, did not look favourably on these new converts, but Wiseman, who had lived long abroad and was more flexible in his ideas, was glad to give his support. This was right and kind, but he did not tend to regard the converts, and Newman in particular, as if they were rare wild beasts caught by him for his own circus. Visitors to Oscott came to look at Newman, Wiseman's catch, and Newman did not like it. Also, Wiseman, who had at first been a little nervous of this great new convert, found that he was a more humble person than he had expected. And then, finding he could be bossed around, he proceeded to boss him around somewhat.

There were, however, compensations, heartwarming things to set against all this. Several of Newman's friends became Catholics about this time. Faber was one. Nice Elizabeth Bowden came into the Church with her children, Charlie, Emily and Marianne, and later on the eldest boy, John, came too. Maria Giberne was another convert, though not an easy one. She was an emotional soul, and every crisis found her in a great state of pother. Newman found her in London, convinced but agitated. He had seen Maria Giberne in such a state before, so he knew what to do. "It is quite easy," he said, and called a cab. He would take her to see a Jesuit. "Not yet!" cried Maria Giberne, as they rolled away towards the terrible priest. But Mr Brownbill, the Jesuit, turned out to be a mild, shy man, with nothing more alarming about him than a pair of large red ears. Later on, when she had finally made up her mind to be a Catholic, she went to make her first confession, and found herself gazing, alarmed, at Mr Brownbill's large, red ear. "Now I shall have to tell all my life to that ear!" she said to herself. She was, however, very happy in her new faith, although she had much grief and trouble from her Evangelical family.

Newman was her great support and gently instanced his own trials when she was most miserable about her own.

"You are, after all, taking your own friends with you," she had said. He told her in reply that he had lost most of his friends. His mother was dead, his sisters were estranged from him. His dear friends Froude and Bowden, who would probably have joined him in the Catholic Church, were dead. Other friends, such as Pusey, who were still alive, were not moving with him. Those young friends he had now, who had come with him, were good friends, but they were removed from him in age. They had been young freshmen at Oxford, or even schoolboys when he was an Oriel don, beginning the Movement, and they knew nothing of his earlier life. But never mind! He had only told all this to Miss Giberne to reassure her, saying at the end that he was sure "God's mercy will make up to you all that you lose, and you will be blessed, not indeed in the same way, but in a higher".

He felt God's blessing very often at Maryvale, especially in the chapel. It seemed very odd, now, that he could have gone to Catholic services in Italy, but without understanding what he saw, and that in his convalescence in Sicily he could have gone into the churches and felt quietened and soothed, but quite ignorant then about the presence of Our Lord in the Blessed Sacrament. Now he said:

> It is such an incomprehensible blessing to have Christ in bodily presence in one's house, within one's walls, as swallows up all other privileges and destroys, or should destroy, every pain.

Later on, he described in a novel he wrote a conversation that some Oxford undergraduates had with a recent convert. He was very quiet about his new beliefs and worship, and they did not realise all he felt until he burst out, in a torrent of fervour:

> To me nothing is so consoling, so piercing, so overcoming, as the Mass, said as it is, among us. I could attend Masses for ever and not be tired.

There is no doubt that Newman was speaking there through his story-book convert.

So Maryvale to him did not mean so much the place where he had to make some rather painful adjustments to a new way of life. It was the place where he first learned what it was to have Christ's bodily presence within one's walls, where he was able "to know that He is close by—to be able again and again through the day to go in to Him", and where he could exult in the Mass that was said in Maryvale chapel every day.

14 — *Rome again*

It was not a long stay at Maryvale, for in September 1846 Newman and Ambrose St John were sent to Rome, to the College of Propaganda, where they would do their final studies for the priesthood. Newman felt like a little boy being sent to school, and he was rather dispirited when a priest informed him of the rules he would have to keep. He would not be allowed to keep his own clothes. St John, hearing this dismal news, said that Newman would make a face when, in the international College of Propaganda, he had to put on a Turkish nightshirt or an American pair of boots. The Rector would read his letters and dole out his pocket-money. Hard rules for an eminent man of forty-five, but he was ready to endure them. The priest, how-ever, was wrong, and the Rector of Propaganda had no intention of treating the new English inmates so.

Newman laid in everything he might need: soap, stick-ing-plaster, braces, needle and thread, steel pens, a spare pair of spectacles, books, envelopes and string are some of the articles on his shopping list. He bought new socks and woollen shirts and underwear. Then he learned that the

Customs might impound new woollen garments. His shirts were already worn, and he determined to make his other woollens look worn too. In London, just before he sailed, he soused his clothes in a pail of water and dried them out the next day. He never told anyone what they looked like afterwards, but Newman probably spent his time abroad in felted socks.

He and St John passed through France where they were kindly entertained, but suffered from the food—fricasséed frogs one day and English roast beef another, "tough in order to be truly à l'Anglaise". They slept restlessly on featherbeds, and longed for the straw mattresses they used to have at Littlemore.

Then they reached Milan and stayed there for a rest in a clear, bright Milanese October, going every day to visit the sumptuous churches in the airy classical style that Newman loved. After Mass every day they went to a "caffe" close to the big cathedral, the Duomo, and had rolls and hot chocolate. Only one thing spoiled their pleasure, the Italian habit of spitting. Newman saw so much that he came to the conclusion that they liked to spit, but one day he saw a man at great pains to clean his coat; to Newman's wicked satisfaction he had, by mistake, spat on his own coat.

There were not only the great beauties of the buildings to see in Milan, the Duomo with its pinnacles snowy white against the blue sky, or the Church of San Fidele "with its polished tall pillars and its smiling, winning altar"; there were also the constant reminders of the saints of that city, dear to Newman already, St Athanasius, St Augustine, St Ambrose. He learned now, for the first time, about another great saint of Milan, St Charles Borromeo, and he thought much of this *Santo Carlo*, a bishop who was greatly beloved by his people, as he walked about.

When they got to Rome, their rooms in the College were not quite ready, so they stayed in a hotel which turned out to be indescribably filthy. It was bad enough in Milan to have had to wash their feet by instalments out of the washbasin, bad enough in France to have had a pie dish and a sugar basin instead of a washbasin and a soap-dish, but to have a carpet that was a nest of fleas and a milk-pail for a slop-pail was really too much!

When they did get into their College they found two rooms and a little adjoining reception alcove made most elegant for their use, with a drawing-room paper on the walls and worked muslin curtains. Newman and St John could have lived a life of ease there, like wealthy tourists, if they had wanted, but they preferred to attend the lectures and fall in with the College rules.

As far as the weather went, they would have had a milder winter in England. Cold and bitter winds blew on Rome; there was the strange sight of orange trees covered with snow, and Newman thought ruefully of the good English fire there would be at Maryvale, with young Walker cracking the coals with a poker. First St John and then he caught dreadful colds.

"Why do you think people come to Rome for their health?" said Newman, speaking thickly and hoarsely.

"I can't imagine," said his friend, pulling up the blankets and rummaging under his pillow for his handkerchief.

The Rector was anxious for their health and comfort. They were bidden not to keep a strict Lenten fast, they were encouraged to make tea every afternoon in their rooms, and when they went down in the morning for breakfast, served from a dirty sideboard rather reminiscent of the Littlemore pig-trough, they found that butter was served for them.

Ambrose St John was anxious to conform with local customs. He learned Italian quickly and was more fluent than Newman. He sallied forth one day and had an Italian haircut, and, to his friend's amusement, was cropped so closely that his hat fell over his eyes. He rejoiced when their new clothes came so that he could look the same as everyone else. Not so Newman. He hated his new clothes and greatly resented the large bill he had to pay for them. For outdoor wear, as clerics in Rome, they had to wear knee-breeches (and Newman always had difficulty in keeping his stockings unwrinkled), a full-skirted coat, with a kind of undergraduate's gown hanging at the back, buckled shoes, and a large, black cocked hat. It was St John's turn to laugh when he saw Newman adjusting his tricorne, grumbling that it was neither ornament nor use, since the wind would blow it off, and growling that to have the pair of them so done up was "like dressing up blackamoors in muslin".

All dressed up, they went to see the Pope, Pius IX, and he was most affable. Newman, bending to kiss his foot, as was the custom then, crashed his head on the papal knee. It is not known which of them suffered most harm. Miss Giberne, who was in Rome too at that time, living in lodgings and painting portraits, did even worse at her papal audience. In a moment of fervour she caught the Pope by the legs and nearly brought him down.

Those were happy days in Rome and yet, as at Maryvale, there was sometimes a little chill in the air. Newman learned that his latest book, *The Development of Doctrine*, was not viewed quite favourably by some Roman theologians, and he got into trouble about a sermon he preached to the English community in Rome; it was a forthright sermon and it was considered tactless.

Moreover, he, who for years, as the leader of the Oxford Movement, had known exactly what work he was about, and had been in a busy, active, fighting mood, now had to endure a time when he simply did not know what God wished him to do in the future. He was to be ordained, but what then? It would probably be best for him and his followers to join one of the Religious Orders, but which should it be? Should they be Passionists like Father Dominic? Or Jesuits like their kind friends and instructors at Propaganda? Or Dominicans?

After much thought and much prayer, Newman reached a very happy decision. Friendship always played a great part in his life, and now he found a new friend, one who was especially near and dear to him. He was St Philip Neri.

St Philip had lived in the sixteenth century, at the time of the Renaissance. He lived in one poor little room, and when he walked abroad in the streets of Rome, a shabby man in his priest's cassock, with a singularly kind face, he looked with sympathy all around him. He saw so many things: the great, new Renaissance churches with their splendid paintings, their new and elaborate music; the jostling Roman crowds in the sunny squares and market places; the poor folk in their rags; the aristocratic Roman youths flaunting themselves in their bright doublets. His wide love included all. He drew people to God by gentleness and humour and he was never pompous, never gloomy. Young men who had never cared much about their religion before found themselves coming to Father Philip's room, talking with him, praying. They came, they stayed, and rather to their own surprise they found themselves not only practising their religion, but actually enjoying it. It was sweet and easy to love God when you were taught by Philip. His own love for God burned like a great fire in his breast.

Only one thing scared him—the thought that other people might reverence him as a holy man. Or worse, he might let self-esteem sprout in his own heart. So he played the fool sometimes in order that he should be despised, and when he thought his young followers were ready to learn humility he gave them a shove into some ridiculous situation. There was a young man who had always been able to give his orders to shopkeepers, for he had rank and money. He would be pleasant but a little grand, handing out tips in a well-to-do-undergraduate fashion. Philip sent him to buy a pennyworth of wine with a large gold piece, and the merchant sent him off with rude words as well as the change, so that the young man's ears burned scarlet.

St Philip gathered other priests about him, and they formed the "Congregation of the Oratory". They did not create a strictly organised Religious Order, but were simply a band of priests living together. Community life held them closely in the affectionate, zealous spirit of their

Father Philip, and just as a good family radiates its warmth and charity to other people outside that household, so each Oratory house would become a centre for all sorts of priestly work for souls.

The more Newman thought about the Oratory, the more he liked its aim and spirit, and he saw how this was a proper continuation of the little community at Littlemore and at Maryvale. And the more he knew of St Philip the more he loved him. Again, the friendship seemed a God-given continuation of old times, for he said St Philip reminded him very much of Keble.

It is surprising that he did not say that his new patron saint reminded him of Hurrell Froude, for he was another person to say that solemn strait-laced pride was fair game. You could kill it in yourself by poking fun at Pharisees; then they either learned to laugh at themselves, which was good for them, or they put you down, out of spite, and that was good for you.

Once a solemn bevy of St Philip's enemies brought a carriage to take him to the mad-house. He learned their intentions and inveigled them into their own conveyance. "To the mad-house!" he cried to the driver, and disappeared indoors, ignoring the angry cries issuing from the carriage windows. How Froude would have enjoyed doing that to a bunch of senior Oxford dons or to a synod of Bishops!

One comparison Newman never saw, though his friends did. There are stories of St Philip that remind one very much of Newman. He questioned a young man about his plans for the future, and the young man, who had no doubt of his own powers, and who had a glorious future quite mapped out, was willing to give an account. He would get his degree and become a successful lawyer, and marry, and earn a lot of money, and . . .

"And then?" asked St Philip quietly.

"Well then, I shall retire in my old age, I suppose."

"And then?"

"Well . . . I shall die."

"And then?"

No more was said than that, but it set the young man thinking. In the same way, Newman by the quietly spoken word and, more still, by what he was, could make ambitious, worldly men think more seriously of the purpose of life. And like St Philip, though he thought people should be serious, he did not think they should be glum.

Newman, who had stiff, shy moods, and who had times when prayer seemed a dry and weary business, would remember Philip's generous ardour for God, and he would think that he was woefully different from his new patron. He said he would not be fit to black St Philip's boots, if they used blacking in Heaven. But there does not seem much doubt that St Philip would value a man who had such humility, and he would go eagerly to meet him as a friend, and bid him put away his blacking-brush.

So Newman made his plans and the Pope gave a glad consent. He would be an Oratorian and found the Oratory in England.

On Trinity Sunday, 1847, Newman and Ambrose St John were ordained priests in the church of the College of Propaganda. Newman said his first Mass on Corpus Christi. He noted both these great events in his diary, but he said nothing whatever about them. He could express himself in writing better than other people, but on such matters he never said anything at all.

All the students at Propaganda came and kissed the hands of the new priests, wished them goodbye and received some medals as keepsakes that Newman had asked Dalgairns to bring over from England. They would miss those two, so much older and so different from themselves, and yet so good-humoured and easy. And it would be odd not to see them about any more, always together, so strikingly different from everyone else and also from each other. Ambrose St John was known as Newman's "Angel" for he was good looking and fair, and looked younger than his years. Newman, however, looked his age and more, though his dark hair had not yet turned grey. The strain of the last years had scored deep lines in his face so that, in repose, he looked stern and sad.

But if St John looked like a grave angel, and Newman like a weary saint, there were times when Newman's face was brightened with laughter and his friend had a most unangelic grin. Newman was the one to start the jokes. He said that the men they collected to start the Oratory had better have a good deal of fun in them too, or otherwise all would be flat and tasteless. "If we have not spirit it will be like bottled beer with the cork out."

Some of his would-be Oratorians were over now from England, and they would all have to go to learn to live by the Oratorian Rule. Once more Newman had to fit himself out with a new style of dress. It was not a big or costly change this time, though—simply a new set of collars. Oratorians wear a black cassock and a soft turned-down collar, quite unlike the stiff Roman kind.

The Pope sent the little band of Englishmen to a house outside Rome called Santa Croce, where they were taught by Father Rossi. He was a dreary man, and on the whole they had a dreary time of it, except for a brief holiday in Naples where they climbed Vesuvius, and bathed, and found on their walks that vines and figs were festooned across the paths, simply asking to be eaten. Also, at Santa Croce, Newman turned his hand to novel writing. His book was called *Loss and Gain*; it was an account of Oxford and religious opinions there, and of the conversion to Rome of one young man called Charles Reding. If Newman worked in his room with the door ajar, passers-by would hear him chuckling as he wrote, and this is not surprising for he put in some good funny parts. One day one of his friends felt compelled to go in to see what on earth Newman was working on that caused him to laugh as he wrote. Why was he writing a novel anyway? It was written out of kindness. Newman had heard that an Anglican gentleman who had been a respected publisher had just been received into the Church with all his family. He wanted to

118

begin again as a Catholic publisher but he needed something to give him a start.

"Poor Burns," said Newman, "a convert like ourselves, has got into difficulties, owing to his change of faith, and I am going to give him this manuscript to see if it may help him a little out of them."

The manuscript did help; James Burns started his Catholic publishing firm straightaway with *Loss and Gain* and his new business continued and continues to this day.

In December Newman and St John set off for England. On the way they visited Loreto where there is the Holy House of Nazareth; there is a legend that angels carried it there from Palestine. Newman stopped there to ask Our Lady's blessing on the new Oratory he was going to found. On they went, then, through the north of Italy to the frontier, and there they met trouble because they had to get a body through the customs. Ambrose St John had acquired the relics of an early martyr in Rome, and eventually the customs men decided it was nothing worse than a mummy, and let it go through! Then the travellers came through Germany and Belgium at speed, crossed from Ostend to Dover and arrived in foggy London on Christmas Eve.

Charlie Bowden was at hand next morning to serve Mass, and he could do it to a nicety since he had always been good at liturgical correctness. Newman, about to begin his new work for God, felt it to be a happy Christmas indeed, a great blessing that he should be able to say his first Mass in England on such a blessed day.

"Introibo ad altare Dei," he began, at the foot of the altar, "I will go up to the altar of God."

"Ad Deum qui laetificat juventutem meam," piped up Charlie Bowden, taking care with his Latin. "To God, who gives joy to my youth."

The Mass went on its swift way. Newman moved and spoke quickly and softly. He came to the Preface, which was the same one he had said for his very first Mass, for Corpus Christi and Christmas are both feasts of the Word made flesh.

. . . Through the mysteries of the Word made flesh
Thy splendour has shone before our mind's eye with a
new radiance, and through Him whom we recognize as
God made visible we are carried away in love of things
invisible.

It expressed the reality that was ever in Newman's
mind, the light of God, Christ Himself, shining in the
darkness of the world.

15 — The Oratory in England

Newman went at once from London to Maryvale. He had
come back to the Midlands to work under Bishop Wiseman. But almost at once Wiseman was moved to London,
and Newman's new Bishop was William Bernard Ullathorne. He was a strong, shrewd little Yorkshireman with
an interesting history; he began life as a cabin-boy and later
became a Benedictine. He was good, and he was talented
and well-suited to be a Bishop, but he never forgot or re-
gretted his humbler days. He did not like nonsense, and he
always dropped his aitches. He was not altogether pleased
to have Newman in his diocese. You can imagine that he
muttered, "So John 'Enry Newman is 'ere, is 'e?" An
Oxford convert, probably smooth and good-mannered, a
bit slippery, and with a good opinion of himself. Later
Ullathorne lost all his distrust and became Newman's
staunch friend, but at first he was not exactly welcoming.

Newman was not out in the country very long. St Philip
had set up the first Oratory in Rome, and it was in the big
cities that Oratorians expected to find their priestly work.
The big city in Newman's own diocese was Birmingham,
and that was where he moved with his little company
before long. A greater contrast to the lovely Oxford where

he had spent his youth could hardly be imagined. Birmingham was the product of the Industrial Revolution, a fast-growing city of factories, its machinery grinding and clanking, its furnaces glowing and roaring. In the centre was a maze of dirty little streets and alleys for the poor factory workers who lived in houses huddled back to back to save space.

Newman found a building that could be turned into a dwelling-house with a good-sized chapel. It was in Alcester Street, in a part called Deritend. "Deritend" sounds in the ears with other similar words such as dirty, dreary and dusty, and well it might to all who know Birmingham. The building had formerly been a gin-distillery, but it could be converted. It had a handsome front for a gin distillery, in classical style. Newman arrived in a "fly" packed with a wonderful assortment of luggage—"a bag of books, a box of rattletraps, loose, a large basket of vials and galleypots, a violin and case, a ditto belonging to Father Richard, a box of relics, a large box containing the Spanish crucifix, a large glass case to go over the same, a plaister Madonna, a plaister Crucifix, a saucer of china shells and the plaister decorated cross from the Guest Room." Later the great crates of books arrived from Maryvale.

Then eventually the other members of the community came, all amongst the building operations, and Newman gave a wonderful description of the resulting chaos:

> There are our members just forming, some coming, some come, everyone taking his place, as one used in a stage-coach, accommodating legs and stowing parcels. You know what a scene there is on deck when a vessel is just under weigh—packages, boxes, mackintoshes, live fowls and qualmish women strewed about in all directions. The school department, the instruction department and the confession department all have to be organized. Then the house is full of masons, carpenters and painters, not to say upholsterers.

Of course (as had happened at Maryvale), some members shirked the dirty work. Father Frederick Bowles took a morning off to read spiritual books, which did not make his brethren feel very spiritual, and later Father John Bernard Dalgairns said piously that he thought an Oratorian should spend his day glued to his confessional. Newman replied that if they all did that, Dalgairns would have no breakfast, no dinner, and would soon have no confessional to be glued to.

When they began services in the new church they expected rows, for Birmingham was suspicious of this new Roman Catholic contingent. Catholics were ill-provided for there, at this time. There was one church, St Peter's, tucked away down a side-street so that it would not offend, and the new cathedral of St Chad placed boldly right in the centre of the city. Pugin had built it in his Gothic style, so that it was full of niches and cornices, and what Newman in his old-fashioned spelling called "skreens". And there was the new Oratory chapel in no style at all. People turned up there in surprising numbers, and there was no attack from "Birmingham roughs". When the priests started evening instructions they were amazed at the crowds of children who began to come. "Boys and girls flow in for instructions as herrings in season," said Newman. They were glad to come in out of the cold and dirty streets, poor ragged children who were out working in the day-time from the age of seven.

Children are now in a good many places where Newman once lived. The Alcester Street building is a school now, so that the shoals still come in. The house at Ham is a day nursery, and small children still play in its pleasant garden. More of a change has taken place at Maryvale for it has become a nursery-school too; three-year-olds are stumping about with toys in the place where Bowles, Stanton, St John and the rest were once struggling with their new theology textbooks.

There was plenty for priests to do in Birmingham, and it was not the most pleasant place in which to work, especially in hot weather. The congregation brought into the chapel the horrid smells of poverty. Newman had once met the attacks of the Italian flea, and now he met a new foe, the Birmingham bug. It took courage to go to hear confessions in the Alcester Street chapel. A priest might come in from the street, which was smelly enough, into the church, where the air was thicker still, and into his confessional box which was the stuffiest of all. There he offered up to God his own longing for some gulps of sweet fresh air, and took his chance that he would catch yet another flea, for they sometimes came hopping through the grille, off the penitent.

Yet Newman had worse things to endure than these. He loved parish work (even in sordid surroundings), and his parishioners loved him. Worse trials came in the setting up of the new community of the Oratory. If only setting up a household, a home, was just a question of moving in the furniture and setting the painters and plasterers to work!—though this is hard enough when there is not much money to do it all. It is creating a true and charitable family spirit that is the hardest thing, since human nature is selfish and wayward.

Now the Oratory is not like a Religious Order with members who take permanent vows. An Oratorian is simply a priest who lives in this community. While he belongs to the Oratory he must keep the Oratorian Rule of course, and he must try to fit in with his fellow-priests in charity and harmony, but, if he decides at any time that this is not his vocation, he may move off. Newman said of their St Philip, "Love is his bond; he knows no other fetter," so he knew what sort of a household a Philippian one should be.

Ordinary homes can be of three kinds: there are the places where there is no discipline or order, and where the children live in a selfish chaos; there are the strict households where there are hundreds of rules, order but little freedom, and where the father thinks his main job is to punish, and there is the home where there are few rules

123

but still there is order and peace because the children have been taught to discipline themselves, and all the family love one another. The third kind is much the best, but it needs a wise father and mother and good children to create it.

Newman was now "the Father" for the new Oratory, and he had to make his household from the beginning. He knew exactly what sort of Father he ought to be. He had to keep order, of course, and see that the Rule was kept (for if they did not keep the Rule which expressed and taught the spirit of their founder they would not belong to St Philip at all) but he had no intention of being heavy handed. Of course the Oratorians acknowledged Newman as their spiritual Father. Ambrose St John solemnly expressed himself in a letter as "your child" and Newman had to laugh, true as the phrase was, for Ambrose was becoming stout, and no longer looked anything like a child, or like an angel. "And a fine babby you are," the Father retorted. But on the whole the new Oratorians were rather a wayward family, unused to obedience, and sometimes conceited. It would have been simpler for Newman to set himself up as a dictator and force them to submission, but this he would not do. Time, patience, prayer to St Philip would make a good Oratorian house in the end.

Some Oratorians came and went, and in some cases the loss was severe. Others came and soon departed because it was obvious that they were quite unfitted for the life. Such was Brother Elkes, a would-be lay-brother, who drank too much beer, and was found laid out on the kitchen dresser. Others came and stayed and did much good as Oratorian priests, and yet they were a trouble too. In particular there was Faber—Father Frederick William Faber. He was a convert and had been an Oxford man and a clergyman like Newman. In his Oxford days he was slim and good-looking, and somewhat sentimental, and he was known as "Waterlily Faber" (after a poem he wrote). When he became a Catholic he started a religious community of his own, and he soon had a good many "brothers" in it, for Faber had an amazing talent for converting people. They all came, when Newman arrived back in England, and offered themselves to him, for Faber thought it would be better to join the Oratory than to go on with their own community. Faber also brought a property with him, a house called St Wilfrid's, at Cheadle in Staffordshire; it had been given to him by Lord Shrewsbury.

Newman used St Wilfrid's as a jumping-off point after they left Maryvale and before they went to Alcester Street, and after that he did not really know what to do with it. There were obstacles in the way of every scheme: living there, selling it, giving it away, shutting it up. Newman was reminded of the unfortunate man who bought an elephant. He was too poor to keep it, and too merciful to kill it, and could not persuade anyone to take it. Eventually the Passionist Fathers bought the house, Newman's own white elephant, and that was that.

But Faber was still to be reckoned with. He (with some of the others, including Dalgairns) viewed matters very differently from Newman. These men were converts of the excitable kind, full of fervour, more Roman than the Romans and more Catholic than the Pope. They thought Newman cautious and stiff and called him "Grandpa" behind his back. Faber's health was a trial too, to himself and others. He was not strong, and he overworked, and in every Oratory crisis, the chances were that he would take to his bed, with spasms, cramps, pains and vomitings, which he described with horrid relish in his letters.

There were too many men for the one house in Birmingham and in 1849 they divided into two lots, Faber taking some people to London to start a second Oratory there. They, too, had a converted gin shop; theirs had been a place for dancing and drinking, not a distillery, and it was in King William Street. Faber got things going in fine style and Newman preached at the opening of the London Oratory chapel to a great concourse of fashionable people. Faber's congregation was much smarter than Newman's.

Later the London house was moved, and it became the

famous Brompton Oratory. The priests there did a great deal of good and Faber in particular was well known, especially for the devotional books he wrote and for his hymns. If you look through a Catholic hymn-book you will find a good many well-known and well-loved hymns that have "F. W. Faber" at the end. He worked on at Brompton until he ceased to be "Waterlily Faber" and became fat and unwieldy through ill health; he lost his youthful looks but he never lost his enthusiasm and spiritual zest.

There was no one like Faber for zeal. He was a good priest and a man who professed himself to be Newman's devoted friend. But it is a sad and strange fact that often one's allies cause more trouble than enemies. Newman had more grief and worry through Faber and the London Oratorians—his own spiritual sons, his fellow Catholics, zealous and apostolic men—than ever he did from those outside the Church. There was a bitter and distressing quarrel between the two Oratories. The cause of it was an application that was made to Rome by the London Oratory to have a clause in the Rule altered. The Roman authorities thought that the application came from both Oratories, and however hard Newman tried to clear up the matter he was left unsatisfied, with a dreadful fear that the Rule might be altered for his Birmingham Oratory without their knowledge or consent. He was also left with the conviction that there had been a deal of intrigue in London.

St Philip's Rule was so important that he journeyed to Rome with Ambrose St John to make sure that the mistake could not be made again, and he felt about the matter so deeply that he suggested, as they neared their journey's end, that they should do penance by walking barefoot to St Peter's over the stones. They would not be noticed for there were few people about, and they were wearing their long "Propaganda" cloaks. He wanted to offer up a sharp penance for his Oratory, as well as prayer at the tomb of the Apostle Peter. Matters were settled in Rome (though Newman had to endure a nasty piece of rudeness from a

Cardinal) and later the two Oratories in London and Birmingham became quite independent. Thereafter Newman kept very quiet and would not allow gossip to damage the London Oratory. They were doing good work and he left them to do it in their own way.

Meanwhile he had plenty to do in Birmingham. They moved out from their gin-shop in Alcester Street to the Hagley Road, a wide, pleasant suburban road where the wealthy "Brummagems" were building houses for themselves. It was an odd neighbourhood for Newman, as odd as smelly Alcester Street in its way, for he did not have much in common with would-be gentlemen who were very set on moneymaking. His new house was a tall, flat-fronted one, and next door he built a church, nice and cheap, with a roof bought ready-made off the top of a factory. At long last his books came to rest on their last shelves, in the library, and upstairs he settled himself into another plain and ordinary room, with a big, shabby desk and an enormous wastepaper basket.

An Oratory house does not exist for its own sake but to be a centre for priestly work. Newman and the other priests said Masses, preached, heard confessions, went visiting, looked after the children in the Poor School, the people in the Workhouse and the Prison. Upstairs, after hours of such work, and having made sure that he had done such jobs as the household accounts, Newman would settle at that desk and work for his own special apostolate.

He wrote out the lectures that he was to deliver, sermons, articles, books. A Lenten series of lectures that he gave in London to please Wiseman turned out a failure, but another set of addresses given later in London was such a glittering success that Newman was given the Roman degree of Doctor of Divinity. These and other works were published in book form and over the years he added to the stack of books he had already written in his Anglican days. Every book was full of careful thought, expressed with a marvellous beauty and exactness, written as if the author had plenty of leisure and no worries.

If he was not writing in this formal way, Newman was writing letters, scores of them, funny ones, descriptive ones, serious ones. When he wrote to advise he seemed to know exactly what each correspondent needed from him, and he always knew exactly the words that would comfort or soothe or strengthen, or chide or teach that person best. Many people wrote to him when they thought they might become Catholics, and they were his special care. Some people needed firmness to help them to make up their minds. Some people were doubtful and perhaps over-excited, and they were told to wait, to be patient. The kind, warm, exact words went down on the paper in his small scholarly handwriting, and he signed them neatly, "John H. Newman". At long last he was done, and he wiped his pen on a penwiper—for a little girl called "Chat", one of his friends, made them for him.

The room, the desk and all, are still to be seen just as they were in the Oratory house which still stands, tall and rather gaunt, on the Hagley Road. The old church has gone, though. A large, fine church has been built there, to replace it, in Newman's favourite style, with Roman pillars. Pugin, who believed that only the Gothic style was religious, would be truly shocked to see such a classical building, such an absence of crockets and skreens. The Oratory church is crowned with a large dome which can be seen (a rather surprising sight) as people approach that area in a Birmingham bus. Newman in certain words kept the spelling and pronunciation that he had learned as a little boy in the earliest days of the century, and he would have called it a "doom". He would be pleased to see that fine "doom" and that church raised to the honour of Our Lady and her Immaculate Conception, and he would be even better pleased to see that the Oratorians are still there, in the church, or dwelling behind those severe, sash-corded windows in the house on the Hagley Road, or in black clerical suits and characteristic turn-down collars, riding by on their bicycles. He brought the Oratory to England, and now it is firmly established here.

But of course the story of Newman's life as a Catholic priest is not simply an account of how he founded the Oratory in this country. As you might imagine, far more exciting things happened to him.

16 – Down with Newman!

In 1850, not long after the start of the two Oratories in England, Wiseman was made a Cardinal and was sent back from Rome to this country to be the first Archbishop of Westminster. Since the Reformation English Catholics had been governed directly from Rome but the time had come for the country to have its own Archbishops and Bishops again. This was "the restoration of the hierarchy". Now Wiseman was an exuberant man who dearly loved a show and a splash. He was delighted, of course, that the English Catholics should have this privilege, and he did not know much about the feelings of Protestants in England. He sent from Rome a pastoral letter to be read from the pulpits, a joyful cry to announce this great event. The pastoral, as Wiseman wrote, was sent "From out the Flaminian Gate", a style of address that set the tone for the whole exuberant and tactless letter. The words sound as if they were meant to be blazoned in letters of scarlet and gold.

This preliminary flourish of trumpets was heard with alarm by non-Catholic England. Obviously the Pope was sending Wiseman as the spearhead of the attack. Queen Victoria would be hurled from her throne, the Inquisition would be set up, and the Pope himself would tyrannise over this Protestant island. This was nicely timed, for Guy Fawkes Day was near. Large guys with red hats on were burnt (Wiseman) or with triple tiaras (the Pope). No Catholic church or house was safe from mob violence, broken windows, mud-slinging. Dreadful stories got around. Whole boatloads of Jesuits were said to be coming up the Thames. A wave of fear passed over the whole country, and children huddled under the bedclothes at night for fear that the Pope would come and get them.

When Wiseman reached England he was filled with surprise and horror to find the situation which he had provoked. He acted speedily and with dignified good sense, and wrote "An Appeal to the English People" which asked for the traditional English fair play, and explained that the restored hierarchy would have nothing at all to do with governing England politically. But most people put down these pacifying explanations as one more example of Popish lies and craftiness.

Newman and the Oratorians came in for a good deal of the attack, because they were so well known. Cartoons of Newman were always coming out in *Punch*, though of course drawings of the wicked Wiseman had first place. In a way, the cartoonists preferred Newman's gaunt face and figure as an example of a miserable monk (Oratorians were *not* monks, but that was a detail) for Wiseman's chubby face looked altogether too cheerful. There were some scuffles in Birmingham, and the rowdies would surge and roar outside the Oratory so that the priest inside could not hear himself preach. A rumour was put about that Newman was married, but had shut up his wife in a convent.

The London Oratory fared rather worse. On Guy Fawkes Day crackers were thrown on the roof of the chapel, while guys of Faber & Co. were burnt outside. Faber called in some policemen to give protection, and provided supper for them at the end of an exciting evening. Outside in the streets were large placards—for instance:

NO POPERY! DOWN WITH
THE ORATORIANS!
NO RELIGION AT ALL!

Faber's men had asked for trouble by going outside in their long cassocks, and the very sight of a long gown filled the mob with fury. One day a Catholic gentleman in a long cloak was followed by a London rabble who took him for an Oratorian. Newman reported, "He faced round, pulled aside the cloke and showed his trousers—when they saw him all sound below they gave a cheer and left him."

Even before the 1850 "Papal Aggression" all the works of Catholics, and especially of priests, and more especially religious superiors, were suspect. One Oratorian was sent by Newman to see a doctor who said darkly, "Have you been through any rigorous course of penances, either self-imposed or put on you by your superiors?"

The young man, whose name was Austin Mills, kept a dead-pan face and said, "Why, *lately* I must say I *have*—"

The doctor looked up eagerly; now he would hear of dreadful doings, tortures and cruelties perpetrated by Father Newman.

Mills finished, "—a severe course of medicine and mustard plasters."

Now, of course, suspicions doubled. It was rumoured that the new house on the Hagley Road had a set of underground dungeons for the Superior to put his monks in if they disobeyed him.

Newman did not leave his countrymen to their fantasies. He gave a series of lectures in the Birmingham Corn Exchange, and tried to puncture the stories with the needle of laughter. He showed how absurd the fears were, and he certainly amused his audience. Ladies were not allowed in to these public lectures, and poor Maria Giberne walked about outside, like a lost soul cut off from the joys of heaven. She could just hear the low tones of Newman's voice, interrupted by ripples of laughter from the audience.

The "No Popery" stories of 1850 can be laughed at because they were so preposterous, and Newman understood this because he had a mild "No Popery" invention of his own to be amused at. Years before, he and John Bowden at Oxford composed a long poem together. It was called

"St Bartholomew's Eve" and it was about the tragic fate of a Protestant gentleman called Julian and a Catholic lady called Florence. The villain of the piece was a cruel priest, inappropriately called Clement. Newman recalled with amusement, "There were no love scenes, nor could there be, for as it turned out to the monk's surprise, the parties had been, some time before the action, husband and wife by a clandestine marriage, known, however, to the father of the lady."

But there was a darker side to the excitement of 1850. There were lies and cruelty and indulgence in sinister imaginings. One man saw his opportunity for gaining fame and money by trading on the popular mood. He was a greasy villain called Achilli, an Italian who had been a Dominican friar. He came to England as a converted Protestant with a collection of anti-Catholic stories that roused further indignation. Newman could not bear that all England should believe his lies. He saw the Devil in all this, he who is the father of lies, and he made up his mind to expose Achilli. It was a courageous action. Newman was always ready to speak up if he thought it necessary. "Speak I must," he had said when the Oxford Movement began, "for the times are very evil, yet no one speaks against them."

He stood up in the Corn Exchange and told the people what sort of a man Achilli was. He imagined the man himself saying:

I am that Achilli who, in the diocese of Viterbo in February 1831, robbed of her honour a young woman of eighteen. . . . I am the son of St Dominic who is known to have repeated the offence . . . at Naples and again in 1840, in the case of a child of fifteen. I am he who chose the sacristy of a church for one of these crimes, and Good Friday for another.

So that was the man whose stories people were believing, and there was the reason why he was no longer a Dominican. Newman spoke plainly about Achilli's offences for this was no occasion for being mealy-mouthed. He had the facts from an article that Wiseman had published in the *Dublin Review*.

He had been left alone, but Newman was accused of libel and had to stand trial. He wrote to ask Wiseman for the evidence he had used for his article, but Wiseman could not put his hand on the relevant papers. In any case he was inclined to believe that the trial would never happen. Newman did not have those important papers until it was too late.

It was necessary to get witnesses from Italy, some of the women that Achilli had wronged, and it would be best to send a woman to persuade them to come.

One day Miss Giberne went to the Birmingham Oratory to go to confession. Afterwards, in the guest-room, she stayed for a chat. Father Newman, leaning against the mantelpiece, eyed her speculatively and said, "I think you can be very useful to us in this affair."

This was Maria Giberne's big moment! Her devotion and loyalty were sometimes an embarrassment to Newman, but they were real. Now she had a chance to do something for him, and she would brave Achilli in person if need be! So up she got, though her knees shook beneath her crinoline.

"I am ready at your service," she said.

Newman explained that she was to go to Italy, if she would, meet Father Joseph Gordon who was there to round up witnesses, and convoy the women home. It was an alarming job for a Victorian spinster lady, aged fifty, but Maria Giberne was nothing if not brave, for all her sentimental effusions, so she packed her bag and went, two days after this invitation.

Her adventures were hair-raising. First the boiler of the ship burst while they were still in harbour, and several people were scalded to death. But this did not deter her; she just took the next boat.

Father Joseph had collected some witnesses, a young woman called Elena, who was with her husband Vincenzo, and a girl from Naples who brought her baby and her grandmother with her. Miss Giberne brought them all as far as Paris, and bore with them patiently. Elena offended Miss Giberne at the start by supposing that she was herself one of Achilli's victims. The party from Naples did not make tactless remarks; their offence was dirt. Miss Giberne bathed the baby herself, when she felt she could not bear it any longer, and cut its verminous hair. It looked much improved.

Elena and Vincenzo she kept pacified by presents. Elena was given a pair of beautiful new stays with front lacings, and a box of magnetic fishes and ducks. Vincenzo, a grumbling man, could only be kept reasonably happy by cigars. Miss Giberne bought him two a day, and she was willing to increase the ration, but Elena would not have it. "Signorina," she said, "there are Three Persons in the Blessed Trinity, but two cigars are enough for Vinci."

Meanwhile, the baby had wet the bed in the Paris lodging house, to the landlady's wrath, and the French maid made such a fuss about sweeping out the Neapolitan's dirty room that Miss Giberne did it herself. Then she went and took a bath, and when she climbed out she found eight fleas that had been washed off her person and were now floating around on the surface. So then she went and had a little quiet weep. But she did not give up. She was determined to keep those Italians in her clutches and get them to England.

And so she did. The Neapolitans were scared of this "heathen country", and Elena would not go out of doors for fear that she might meet Achilli lurking for her. But Vincenzo went out, to Miss Giberne's relief, for he was the biggest nuisance of them all. He walked about London and could not think who was the saint on top of the column in Trafalgar Square.

In the meantime, Newman was going through months of anxiety and suspense, enduring the slow processes of the law. At last the trial took place.

There was a mass of evidence against Achilli: docu-

ments from the Roman Ecclesiastical Court that had found
him guilty of immorality; Elena and the girl from Naples
to testify; other girls who had suffered from Achilli in
England, including one who had had a baby by him.
Achilli stood up in court, an unpleasant-looking customer,
as even his supporters thought, with a narrow, receding
forehead and little dark, crafty eyes. He denied every
charge without a tremor, without a tinge of colour coming into his sallow cheeks. It was his word against Newman's, but although Newman had a mass of proof that he
had said nothing except the strict truth, it was he who was
proclaimed a liar, and not Achilli. Judgment was brought
against him, and loud cheers went up in the courtroom at
the verdict. That would serve the Papists right!

Miss Giberne had sat at home, minding the Italian baby
and praying that the trial would not go amiss. When she
heard the bad news she cried a little, but then she bestirred
herself to swift action, for she had to get her tribe back to
Italy again. Father Joseph came with her, so it was not too
difficult.

Achilli had won, but it was an empty triumph. The next
day *The Times* published an article expressing great un-
easiness about the trial. How could England deal with the
Roman Catholic problem if the Catholics could justly com-
plain that they were treated very unfairly? English fair
play had not been used, and thinking people were ashamed.
Achilli slipped away, and was never seen in England again.

Newman's friends were deeply distressed by the verdict,
but he himself was not too perturbed. He had expected
that the trial would go against him. He did not think he
had been rash or unwise in speaking out against Achilli,
for he had prayed and considered long and carefully before he spoke, and he thought God was using him, and now
purifying him by this suffering. He had to wait months
before he heard his sentence. It was thought likely that he
would be sent to prison, and his doctor was really afraid
that he would not survive the experience. His friends were
horrified. Imagine Newman in jail, sewing mailbags with

the Bill Sykes types of the criminal underworld. The idea would be funny if it were not tragic. Newman himself remained very calm. He spent long periods of time praying before the Blessed Sacrament, and he often murmured the prayer that, it is said, St Andrew uttered as he saw the instrument of his coming martyrdom:

"O good cross, cross that I have long desired."

Kind letters came in continually from Catholics promising their prayers. Newman had recently made friends with some Dominican nuns at Stone in Staffordshire. Their Congregation had not long been founded by Bishop Ullathorne and by Mother Margaret Hallahan, a stout, forceful, holy woman who had once been a servant girl. She had a great regard for Newman, and he for her. Her letters were a tonic, sometimes a fierce one. When he had maintained that he would suffer defeat in the trial, she trounced him soundly in a kind way. He was to have more confidence and Our Lady would see him through. He was right in thinking that there would be defeat to endure—but he agreed with Mother Margaret that, looking at the events as a whole, again Our Lady was not unmindful of him.

At last Newman was summoned to hear the worst. He was all ready for prison if need be, and he had made arrangements to say Mass there. There was every reason to have a second trial, the lawyers said, but this application was refused. So now, at long last, Newman was called into the court to hear his sentence. He stood in the centre and listened to the judge's harangue. For half an hour Judge Coleridge told Newman how he had gone from bad to worse since he had become a Catholic. He used to be a bright light as a Protestant, and, said the interfering old judge, turning up his eyes with a heavenly look, "O Mr Newman, then I loved your meek spirit." But now he had become, as a result of his conversion, mean, malicious, proud and coarse. Newman was not too much perturbed by this public, shaming lecture; he said afterwards that he had had to endure so much criticism in his time that he was like a skinned eel that could feel the pain no longer.

At the end of this, Judge Coleridge did *not* send him to prison, but fined him one hundred pounds. Perhaps he did not dare do more. The fine was paid, and Ambrose St John and other friends hustled Newman out of the court to find two hundred Irish Paddies just outside cheering themselves hoarse. Even if he did maintain that he was a skinned eel now, and humiliation did not hurt him, he had had much to suffer, and the long, long months of anxiety and suspense had been very hard and wearing.

The hundred pounds paid as a fine was a drop in the ocean of costs. There was the money to be paid for keeping the witnesses so long—and who could blame the landladies if they put extra on the bills they presented to Miss Giberne?—and there was the heavy cost of the long legal process. Catholics subscribed to a fund to help Newman, and they collected an enormous amount of money, over and above what he needed. He was even more pleased to have their warming sympathy and good will. It did not matter to him much that respectable society had written him off as a most unrespectable person. Once it was "the thing" to go to St Mary's to hear him preach, but now he was strictly avoided by most society people. Fashionable ladies swished their great skirts and hissed and muttered: "My dear! Such a sordid business! Fancy his mixing himself up in such a matter, and saying those dreadful things!" All this touched him very little. He thought more of the comfort and gratitude he was having from his own brethren in the Catholic Church, from Bishop Ullathorne down to the Paddies.

Cardinal Wiseman, too, was full of sympathy. When he heard that Newman had been found guilty he was amazed and very grieved, for he had a hopeful spirit and a kind heart. He spent a sleepless night tossing about, thinking of Newman, and then he wrote to him to send his sympathy. To do something positive, he asked him to accept the honour of preaching at the assembly of the new Bishops, the Synod, that was to be held at Oscott.

So in July 1852, between the verdict and the sentence (for he was kept waiting a whole seven months between times), Newman laid aside his own distresses and mounted into the high pulpit in Oscott's Gothic chapel to speak to that great assembly. His sermon was, of course, about the restoration of the hierarchy, the return of the Catholic faith to England. Once it had flourished in this country, but for centuries a hard cold winter for the Catholic Church had made it seem that it could never rise again here in full life and vigour. Now there was a "Second Spring". This sermon was as beautiful as any that Newman preached, clear and flowing, intensely felt by him and by those who heard it. He did not show that he was undergoing nerve-wracking experiences, pressed and harassed by legal business and with the prospect of prison before him. Yet his poetic song of sober triumph for the "Second Spring" in England had much to do with his own life. God would prevail, whatever troubles came. The Church was attacked now in England, and once it had well-nigh dwindled away in this country, but there would always be springtimes of hope and renewal for her. Who could speak of hope and faith, and who could be both serene and alive to the realities of evil? Surely it was Newman—the man who was suffering for the Church, who had borne the attack and was feeling the hurt of it at that very moment.

Wiseman, who loved great occasions, looked round Oscott chapel with satisfaction. The sermon had moved all that congregation, and since they thought it no shame to cry, there were tears in their eyes. Wiseman himself rubbed away tears from his broad cheeks; he was having a good cry. and really enjoying it. Round about him he had his new Bishops, in splendid ranks. Up there in the pulpit was one of England's finest preachers, speaking in that low, sweet, unforgettable voice, making his curious, long pauses. And the man was a convert, one of the many there would be, please God, in this new English spring of the Roman faith. Converts? There was another distinguished recent convert here to-day, a man that Wiseman liked and admired, more than he did Newman. He looked across at a man called Manning.

You could not miss Henry Edward Manning in any crowd. His face and head were remarkable. He had a large, bald, clever forehead, a tight, small mouth, and fine, grey, luminous eyes. He was handsome, splendid, austere—and rather terrifying. Wiseman was quite right to think that he would make his mark and do much for the Church in England. He was destined to be the next Archbishop of Westminster. He was also to be Newman's implacable enemy.

17 − Across the Seas to Ireland, and back again

In seven years Newman crossed to and from Ireland fifty-six times, winters and summers; when the sea was calm and the wind blew fresh and pleasantly, and sometimes in the greatest discomfort, the boat lurching and the passengers suffering from "topsiturvies of the stomach". He had to whisk over to Ireland and then back again right in the middle of the Achilli business, just to add to his fatigue.

He did this because he had been invited by the Irish Archbishop Cullen to be the Rector of a Catholic University in Dublin. The whole thing was starting from scratch. Newman would have to plan it all, find the lecturers, draw up timetables, organise the finances and find the buildings. It was a scheme after his own heart. To seek after knowledge, first the knowledge of God and then human knowledge in all its fascinating variety had been his aim ever since his father's hired chaise had carried him into Oxford's lovely streets for the first time, and to give knowledge to others had always been his task and his joy. He planned a University that would borrow Oxford's ways and methods and yet be up-to-date, with a sound medical school and opportunities for the scientific learning that was rapidly becoming so important. It should have the best of the old and of the new. He hoped that it would be a centre of learning for the Irish and the English, and perhaps for men from the colonies too, and even from America.

So he came. First he stayed in lodgings and suffered agonies from Irish maids and shopkeepers, and from his own inability to stamp and roar and get what he wanted. He bought himself a packet of "villainous tea" which kept him awake for hours; he did not think there was one true leaf in it, though the man who sold it to him was "very great about it". His housekeeper turned his room upside down, arranging all his papers and all his linen according to a method of her own; she sorted them according to size. When he travelled around he always suffered greatly from two items of Irish hospitality, the undercooked meat and the feather beds. When he saw yet another great joint of meat put in front of him, and saw it "blush" as the carving knife and fork went into it, he felt quite ill and would beg for more common meat—bacon; and after nights of sleeplessness on hot, smothering feathers he asked for a hard mattress. The Irish were most impressed with his "mortifications" and provided more underdone beef and softer beds. They nearly killed him with their kindness.

He went up and down Ireland to meet the Bishops and gain support for the University. Most of them had no intention of giving it any support at all, but they made Newman very welcome for they liked him. During these roamings he had some of his funniest adventures. He dined at Carlow with a party of priests, and fell asleep in the middle of the meal. He was wakened by his neighbour on the right shouting, "Gentlemen, Dr Newman is about to explain to you the plan he proposes for establishing the new University."

He then went on to Kilkenny where the carman put him down at the Protestant Bishop's house, not the Catholic one. He rang and rang, with no reply, but at last the scullery-maid came and told him where he was, and that the Bishop was away. This was perhaps a mercy, because the Bishop was a great Newman-hater. The Catholic Bishop laughed heartily when he heard of this incident and said he was not surprised that Newman had been taken for a travelling Protestant in the cloak he had on. The truth was that Newman had left his "good Propaganda cloke" behind, so he went to an Irish tailor's to buy a new one. The man offered him a loud shepherd's plaid. "But it is not clerical?" said Newman doubtfully. The man, sizing up his customer correctly, assured him that it was, so Newman bought it, and was left, as he said, to wander "over the wide world in a fantastic dress like a Merry Andrew, yet with a Roman Collar on".

His own account of his visiting a girls' school at Waterford and falling out with the nun headmistress is best told in his own words. He said in a letter to the Oratory that he would relate:

how he went to the Ursuline convent there, and the Acting Superior determined he should see all the young ladies of the school to the number of seventy, all dressed in blue with medals on, some blue, some green, some red; and how he found he had to make them a speech and how he puzzled and fussed himself what on earth he should say impromptu to a parcel of schoolgirls— and how in his distress he *did* make what he considered his best speech—and how when it was ended the Mother School Mistress did not know he had made it or even begun it, and still asked for his speech. And how he would not, because he could not, make a second speech; and how, to make it up, he asked for a holiday for the girls, and how the Mother School Mistress flatly refused him, by reason (as he verily believes) because she would not recognise and accept his speech, and wanted another, and thought she had dressed up her girls for nothing—and how he nevertheless drank her raspberry vinegar, which much resembles a nun's anger, being a sweet acid, and how he thought to himself, it being his birthday, that he was full old to be forgiven if he would not at a moment act the spiritual jack-pudding to a girls' school.

Eventually Newman set up house at 6, Harcourt Street, Dublin, and had some of the new students there with him. One of them was especially anxious to be there and away from home. He was accustomed to take hot milk with a little bread for his breakfast, he wore a "spencer" for extra warmth, and when he went out at home two aunts always accompanied him, one walking before and another behind, in case he should collapse. The house soon became a home, with Newman to preside over it. He, of course, was very busy in it, taking on small but tiresome jobs that other people were too lazy or too incompetent to do. There was the carving to be done for instance, since his assistant could not take the wing off a chicken without turning the bird upside down; and the locking up, because the servant forgot it. He made many friends in Dublin, and they came in for visits, one young layman writing with enthusiasm of the "comfortable cose" he had had with Newman, with port wine and biscuits and chat of Oxford days. But he did not succeed in renewing his old friendship with Whately who was near at hand as Archbishop of Dublin. He sent a chilly note to say that he was "not at home". Perhaps when Newman went out for walks he sighted Whately from afar, on occasion, exercising his dogs in some green open space in Dublin.

Newman set about providing for his students in every way, and he saw to it that they had recreations as well as studies. They went out riding, joined the Debating Society he had started, and never had to put up with niggling rules, or an under-lock-and-key policy from the Rector. Remembering the old billiards room at Ham, where his father taught him the game when he was very small he set up a billiards room for his students too.

Archbishop Cullen was most surprised. To his mind, a Catholic University should be a stricter place, more like a seminary for training priests. He would not encourage the billiards. In fact, and very curiously, since Newman had only come on his invitation, he was not encouraging at all. When Newman was in Birmingham making the first arrangements he sent off letters to Dr Cullen asking important questions and was met with silence. Cullen was having his difficulties with the Dublin University for he was mightily opposed by another Archbishop, John Mc-Hale, Archbishop of Tuam, known as the Lion of the West. The Lion was always lashing his tail at Cullen, and he would have liked to have got his paws on Newman too. Cullen's policy, when in difficulty, was to keep very quiet and not to answer letters. Newman was a disappointment to him. He had hoped for a mild scholar, a venerable figurehead to set up over the new University, which Dr Cullen wanted there as a kind of monument of opposition to the colleges that had been set up by the British Government, where Catholics and Protestants would study together. But Newman was so very active. His idea of a Catholic University was positive, splendid and vital. Dr Cullen found it positively alarming.

At one point it was suggested that Newman should be made a Bishop so that he would have more authority and weight as University Rector. Newman was not out for honours, but he would have welcomed any strengthening of his hand, and he waited for the promised bishopric to come. His friends were delighted and sent him suitable presents; a great morse or clasp for a cope came, and a pectoral cross, the kind gift of Mrs Bowden. But the bishopric never came. To be offered an honour and then not receive it, when all the world had heard of the coming promotion, was a humiliation indeed. At this time Miss Giberne had a private audience with the Pope and said to him, plainly, in her no-nonsense way, "Holy Father, why don't you make Father Newman a Bishop?" The Pope gave no answer, looked confused, and took a great deal of snuff.

Newman forgot the snub as quickly as he could and went on working for the University, getting together a team of professors and lecturers, mostly laymen.

But it was hopeless. The Irish were busy opposing the English and also one another. The English had no intention of sending their sons across to Ireland. In Ireland there were few laymen willing to support the new University, and indeed it is hard to blame them since any degrees issued there would not be recognised by the government. There was a chronic shortage of money. After seven years of frustration, Newman resigned.

All that labour has not vanished without a trace. He left one memorial in the form of a University church. He had built it himself, out of his surplus "Achilli Case" money that the Catholics had subscribed. It is a far finer church than his cheap Birmingham church was, domed and classical, with frescoes of Our Lady, Seat of Wisdom, who of course is the patroness of a Catholic University.

He also left a book called *The Idea of a University* which is a collection of addresses he made, the lectures given before the University was even established, and other later ones. He defined a Univeristy, its purpose and scope, and showed how human knowledge should be related to Christian faith. It is a large, deep subject, and one that will never cease to be important. Newman had important things to say here, and he said them supremely well. He would be a rash man, nowadays, who claimed to know about Universities or about education in general and who did not know something of Newman's theories, had never read a page of his clear and eloquent arguments. So perhaps it was worth that thankless striving, if only for this. It is doubtful whether Newman would have written his thoughts on education if he had not had the actual creation of a University on hand, since he usually wrote when occasions demanded that he should take up his pen. We may feel consolation in the thought—but for Newman, at the time, there was only the bitterness of defeat.

He came back to England to stay, thankful at least that he did not have to go on leading a double life, keeping both the Dublin University and the Birmingham Oratory going. Soon he set about another, smaller educational venture. He did it himself, no one else providing the suggestion this time, and after some perils, some difficulties within and attacks and criticisms without, this venture succeeded.

He started a school, a boarding school for about seventy boys, housed next door to the Oratory itself. It opened on May 2nd 1859, the feast of St Athanasius, and also young Herbert Mozley's birthday. (He probably knew nothing of his Uncle John's project, for the Mozleys were keeping at arm's length.) St Athanasius and St Philip blessed the school, and it prospered.

Some Catholic schools were for training boys towards the priesthood. Newman hoped that one day some young Oratorians would be coming from his school, but it would be run for ordinary boys who would have to go out into the world as well-educated, good, alert laymen. It was an unusually mild and pleasant school for those times. Anxious mammas could send small boys there without fear that they would get cuffs and thrashings, coarse food and small beer. Careful papas were not fond of sending their sons to Birmingham, a most ungentlemanly place, but Newman's name and the good scholarship of the Oratory School won them to the idea. Many of the boys who came were the sons of converts.

At one time the school was rocked to its foundations by a dispute between Newman and the headmaster. Newman reorganised the place, the headmaster went, and Father Ambrose St John was appointed instead. He was supported by lay masters and by the Matrons, who were important in that homelike establishment. There was a Mrs Wootten who was in charge, a gentle lady, who provided strengthening glasses of wine and rides in a carriage for boys who

"He preached to the boys"

had been ill, and there was Miss Mitchell, who looked so gay and youthful that Father Newman had doubts of the wisdom of appointing her. "You will have trouble," he said darkly, looking at her ringlets. But Miss Mitchell said she was not as young as all that, and would wear a cap over her curls, so she came and managed to preserve both order and jollity.

Newman did the examining himself, and though he was kind, he did not put up with shoddy work so, if you were a boy at the Oratory School, you took care with your Latin, Greek and Mathematics or you might find yourself outside Father Ambrose's study for a painful reason. Boys met Newman on happier occasions than examining days, however. He adapted classical plays for their use, and coached them in their parts, showing an extraordinary verve and talent when he did so. He was remembering how much he had enjoyed

> ... the glad auspicious day
> The Doctor tells us we may have a play,

when he himself was a boy at Dr Nicholas' school in Ealing. Also he started a school orchestra where he played second fiddle, sawing away next to the boys, and enjoying it as much as anyone.

He preached to the boys too. They remembered in after years how he had his hands on a Bible as he preached, and how he read from it, reading out a line and then pausing, almost as though he was listening to the words more than he was giving them out to his congregation. Unselfconsciously he listened for the word of God, and by his reverent manner he probably taught more than he did even in his wonderful sermons.

When Newman became a very old man the school was going strongly. The same friendly relationship was there between the Father and the schoolboys. They made him a birthday present of some candlesticks, and his answer expresses the gentleness and simplicity he had in his famous days.

To the Boys of the Oratory School.

My Dear Boys,

You could not have made me a more opportune present than you made me on my birthday, since hitherto my altar candlesticks have been borrowed from the sacristy.

One or two of you should come and see how well they look in their place.

And I want in turn to make your Library a present of some of my books, when I learn what you have already.

And now I give you my blessing: it is the blessing of an old man who is soon to go. Your life is opening:— May God be with you as he has been with me, and He will be with all who seek Him.

Yours affectionately,
JOHN H. Card. NEWMAN.

March 12, 1884.

The difference in age did not lessen the affection and regard the boys had for Newman or he had for them. On one occasion, however, the difference did lead to a very small disagreement. One boy, near the top of the school and feeling himself exceedingly grown-up, had a letter from Newman. He noticed approvingly that the old man had addressed him as "Esq.", on the outside. But, alas, it was a slip of the pen, and Newman in the letter bade the boy apologise on his behalf to his Mama for "his making a little man of him". It was a blow.

In later years the Oratory School was moved, and the original school buildings were taken over by a Grammar School. St Philip's Grammar School still flourishes next to the Oratory. The Oratory School is now at Woodcote near Reading, a growing public school. It is no longer attached to the Oratory, but of course Newman is still venerated there as the Founder.

Perhaps University colleges in Ireland still owe something to Newman. Perhaps the Oratory School still bears something of his imprint. It is certain, however, that education in England has never been quite the same since Newman thought and wrote and worked for it. He has left his mark.

18 — *The Book of Job*

When he was young Newman kept a journal or diary. Later he discontinued it, but he did have a book in which he made jottings from time to time. He thought of Job who suffered patiently and yet made his complaints. He could hardly imitate the Patriarch Job, sit on a dunghill and scrape himself with a potsherd, but he did write down his most sorrowful thoughts from time to time. In this way he relieved his mind and did not burden his friends with his griefs.

His one great grief, his cross, was this: that in his life as a Catholic he was able to do so little. There was so much to do, and he had powers to use but, however hard he tried—and he was never idle—most of his projects came to nothing. They were troubled times and men of faith had much to accomplish. As Newman had seen at the time of the Oxford Movement, the tide of "liberalism" was rising higher, and religion was attacked in all quarters. As far as the Roman Catholic Church in England was concerned, though it was a time of growth and vitality, it was also a time of difficulty. The Archbishops and Bishops, with no tradition to follow in England since the Hierarchy had only just been restored, had their work cut out to lead their flock, because the flock was made up of very different kinds of sheep. There were rich and poor, new converts and old families, English of the English, and Irish immigrants, learned and uneducated. There were differences of opinion that led to wranglings.

Newman believed that a most necessary work was what he called "the edification of Catholics" and by that he meant that they should be better educated, encouraged, laity as well as clergy, to come with fresh, vigorous minds and strong faith to the problems of the day. A hundred years afterwards Pope John XXIII said at the start of the Second Vatican Council that the Church must renew herself, return to the spirit of the Gospels, show herself in all her strength and beauty, ready to face all the difficulties of the modern age, and then others outside the Church, seeing her as she really is, would be drawn to her. Of all the men who lived a century before, John Henry Newman was the one who would most applaud that utterance.

This, he thought, was the way to bring in converts, but here Wiseman and Faber disagreed with him. They believed in a vigorous campaign for bringing in converts in shoals. Newman admired their zeal—but he did wish he was allowed to get on with his own work, on his own lines, without snubs and interference.

His Book of Complaints only contained brief references to all the circumstances that led to his being so thwarted. It would be interesting if he had left us another, fatter book which gave a real chronicle of all those happenings. The best we can do is to reconstruct them briefly.

The first, major setback was, of course, the failure of the Catholic University in Ireland. A few years later a new piece of work was offered to Newman, and it seemed that it was just the thing for him. It was to supervise an English translation of the Bible. At Cardinal Wiseman's invitation Newman began the task, and got his translators and assistants together. But there was no further word from Wiseman; he did not answer letters, he did not offer any solution to the problem of where the money was to come from to pay for the project. Eventually news came from America that a translation was to be made there. Newman thought he might join forces with the team in Baltimore, but Wiseman would not say yea or nay. So Newman regretfully laid aside his translation and the Americans carried on.

Perhaps Wiseman had some excuse for that amazing silence for he was growing ill and muddly and old before his time. The whole matter is something of a mystery. It is certainly enough to make Englishmen gnash their teeth with rage now. What did we lose when we lost a translation of the Bible by Newman? He knew and loved the Scriptures as few men do, and he was a master of English prose. But he did not carry through this work because he was not allowed to do it.

The next trouble was a scuffle over a paper called the *Rambler*. It was run by two young men called Acton and Simpson, who were a hot-headed pair without tact or moderation, who often wrote or put in articles which annoyed the Bishops. The Bishops, who knew that Newman was a friend of theirs, asked him to restrain them, and they handed the editorship to Newman. They passed on the baby, in fact, and a very troublesome baby it was.

Further exception was taken to the *Rambler* by a phrase of Newman's own about "consulting" the faithful in matters of doctrine. He did not mean that the Pope and the Bishops should ask the opinions of laypeople before they taught; he spoke of "consulting" as one might speak of consulting a barometer. He meant that the Bishops should find out what the body of the faithful did believe on any disputed point. Even Ullathorne, so shrewd and moderate a man, thought Newman supported the laity too strongly. "What are the laity?" he said in disparaging tones.

Newman said the Church would look foolish without them.

The Bishops got Newman to hand back the *Rambler* to Acton and Simpson. He would neither disobey the Bishops nor disassociate himself entirely from his friends. So now he was well mixed up with all the *Rambler's* business, and anything unwise in it would be attributed to him, but he could not be fully responsible for its articles since he was no longer the editor. The *Rambler* got into scrapes and got Newman into scrapes until the day it was ended.

Meanwhile Newman had written and published in this ill-fated monthly a whole article called "On Consulting the Faithful in Matters of Doctrine". It was actually sent to Rome as heretical. The authorities at Rome did not attack Newman and his article publicly (when he could have made a straight defence). All the negotiations were done through Wiseman, and he did as little as possible. So Newman's reputation was tarnished in Rome.

In 1865 Cardinal Wiseman died and had a splendid funeral; it is a great tribute to him that many English people paid their respects, even those who were out for his blood when he first came as Archbishop of Westminster.

The new Archbishop was Manning. Ward, the clever, fat man, was as given to enthusiasms as he had been in his Oxford days. He was a great friend of the new Archbishop, and when he heard of Pius IX's choice he rushed about the house, waving his telegram, knocking the chairs down and shouting, "Henry Edward, by the grace of God and favour of the Holy See, Archbishop of Westminster!"

Newman was to have three enemies, and they formed a curious trio. He called them the Three Tailors of Tooley Street. One was Manning, one was Ward, and the third was a priest called Monsignor Talbot, who lived in Rome. He was a stout and snobbish man with two chins, a bland bald forehead and a pursy mouth. It was his delight to go from Pope to Cardinal and back again, retailing the gossip and ministering to his own sense of power. He was a sort of Vatican Golightly. Newman was in ill-favour in Rome, and Talbot's little machinations did not help.

Newman fell out with Talbot first of all when the Monsignor was being affable. He called at the Oratory when he was in England. Newman was away, but Father Austin Mills, who was a good hand at dealing with nosey-parkers, came to receive him.

"Does Father Newman read?" said Monsignor Talbot, hoping this would open up some avenue of exploration.

"I know he takes books out of the library," said Father Austin solemnly, preserving a give-nothing-away face.

Talbot wrote to Newman, offering him preaching in Rome, as an exchange for ministering to the nasty Brummagems. Newman's eyes were blue steel, and his big mouth was set in an uncommon grimness when he wrote his reply. He sent off one of the best snubs ever penned:

> The Oratory, Birmingham.
> July 25, 1864.

Dear Monsignore Talbot,—I have received your letter inviting me to preach next Lent in your Church at Rome to "an audience of Protestants more educated than could ever be the case in England."

However, Birmingham people have souls, and I have neither taste nor talent for the sort of work which you cut out for me. And I beg to decline your offer.

> I am, yours truly,
> JOHN H. NEWMAN.

This was, in fact, asking for trouble, and Talbot, in a quiet way, supplied it. He never actually succeeded in giving Pope Pius IX a personal dislike of Newman, and Newman kept an affection for the Pope, though he did not like all his policies. Of course, his obedience to the Pope was absolute; he would have given this in any case.

Manning was a truly important person, not a man who had to pretend to be so, like Talbot. He was clever, charming, skilful in handling men and affairs. He cared for the Church and its advancement with all his heart and soul, and he was prepared to put all his considerable strength, energy and ability to supporting what he thought was right. He was a great Archbishop of Westminster, and his greatest claim to fame is a splendid one, that he cared for the poor and was energetic in social reforms.

He worked mightily, sitting in his plain room—for he had no love for riches or comfort—and occasionally startling visitors by calling out "Newman! Bring some more coals for the fire!" No, he did not keep the Superior of the Birmingham Oratory there in bondage, carrying the coal scuttle. Newman was the name of his butler.

Manning was a formidable opponent, and he never had doubts about his own opinions. If you disagreed with him, you disagreed with the Church, and he would crush you if he could. He, too, was always conscious of the difficulties of the time, knowing that new industrial power, new techniques, new scientific learning made men restless; he knew of the great rise against religion. Newman thought the answer was to meet the new age with its own weapons. He longed for a really educated laity. He valued obedience —no man more—but he wanted obedience to be vital and intelligent. Manning thought that in evil times authority should be strengthened more and more.

Their first big clash came over a project that was put forward more than once, that nearly succeeded. It was suggested that another Oratory should be set up at Oxford, and that Newman should return there. Catholics had originally been debarred from entering the University; now, although the University would admit them, they could not go there in conscience because the Bishops, under Manning, were for keeping them away. They thought that Oxford, liberal, free-thinking Oxford, was a danger spot, and young men would lose their faith there. Newman did not want to go back for his own sake, lured by the memory of the Oxford bells, longing to return when he saw the famous spires from the railway. It would not be easy to return like a ghost to the place where Hawkins still ruled at Oriel, where Pusey, his former companion, was still esconced. But Oxford people had souls too, and this was a work he could well do. He went so far as to buy pieces of land to build the Oxford Oratory on, but at the last moment he was stopped. Ullathorne, Newman's Bishop, was instructed by the authorities at Rome to see to it that Newman did not go to Oxford; if he tried, he was to be restrained "blande suaviterque", gently and smoothly. He was to be buttered, and the best butter was to be used.

Newman knew perfectly well that Manning was determined that young men should not go to Oxford, and he was even more determined that Newman should not go there. No doubt he thought that once Newman was settled there the young and intelligent would be round him, like flies round the honeypot.

There was one thing to be said for W. G. "Ideal" Ward, that he never used a quiet, buttering treatment. He might, metaphorically, sling a brickbat, but there was no doubt where the missile had come from. He and Manning joined forces over a matter of opinion. The subject was the position and the power of the Pope. At this time Italy was in a state of turmoil, Garibaldi was abroad with his revolutionaries, and the Papal States were being wrested from the Pope. Before long the whole matter would be settled, and the Pope would no longer be an earthly sovereign, except over the tiny area of the Vatican. He would lose what is known as the "Temporal Power". Now Manning and Ward, and Faber too, in his day, held most strongly that it was a dreadful matter that the Pope should lose the Temporal Power, whereas Newman had a notion that he would be able quite well to do without it. Oh, shocking! Newman, who was "worldly" in his views on education, "heretical" in his writing, was now "disloyal" too.

When the First Vatican Council was convened it was decided that the dogma of the Pope's infallibility should be defined. Some clamoured loudly for the definition and held somewhat exaggerated opinions about the scope of the Pope's infallibility. Ward, in his exuberant way, said that he hoped, after the definition, that he would be able to come to breakfast every day and find a fresh piece of infallible teaching from the Pope on his table. Definitions would come as regularly as the newspapers. Such extremists were known as "Ultramontanes".

Newman was not an Ultramontane. He had no doubt that the Pope was infallible, but he thought that the definition of the dogma could wait, and that the views of Ward and Manning were extreme. They claimed to speak with the very voice of the Church, but he thought they were raising their own opinions to divine status. The next thing that happened was that a story got around that Newman was in fact a revolutionary, a follower of the godless Garibaldi. It is a mercy that photography had not been invented in the eighteen thirties, and that no photograph was extant of Newman when he was about to set out for the interior of Sicily, sitting on a mule and wearing a foreign straw hat. People's worst suspicions would have been confirmed.

In 1870 the dogma of the Pope's infallibility was solemnly defined. The Council had some turbulent scenes, and tempers occasionally rose among the venerable Bishops.

A man who held, somewhat heretically, that power should be vested locally and not in the central authority of the Pope was known as a "Gallican". An Italian Bishop used the term of Ullathorne. That worthy clambered over the benches until he was cheek by jowl with the speaker. "You call me Gallican?" said he, and (Ullathorne reported it himself) "I fixed him with my glassy eye." The Italian Bishop fell back in confusion and Ullathorne clambered back to his place.

At last the Pope spoke the solemn words, declaring that every Pope, when "as Shepherd and Teacher of all Christians he defines a doctrine concerning faith or morals to be held by the whole Church" cannot utter what is wrong. At the very moment the Pope spoke, a big thunderstorm was breaking overhead; there were great cracks of thunder and darkness, interspersed with vivid flashes of lightning. England heard all about it from the pen of Tom Mozley, who was at that time the Rome correspondent for *The Times*.

Inasmuch as the definition had been made then, and not left to some later date, Manning and the Ultramontanes had won. But there was nothing extravagant in the terms of the definition, no hope at all for Ward's breakfast table. You might say that Newman had won too.

Never for one moment did Newman regret his conversion. He was sure, content, serene, and any suggestion that he was not entirely convinced and utterly loyal brought a sharp rejoinder from him. But his Catholic life was a hard one. Life with other Catholics did not mean joining a kind of club where all felt and thought alike. The Church now seemed like a great net where fishes of many sorts lay together. The parable of the fishes in the net is a parable of judgment, for ultimately the good and the bad fish are sorted out. But without judging, without saying who is good and who bad, you can see the net as the great container of diversities. There were two fat fish—Ward and Talbot. There was a great fish, a fine fellow with gleaming metallic scales and powerful muscles to lash his tail—Manning. And there was Newman next to them, a willing prisoner in the Lord's net.

There were so many ways in which he could have gone wrong. He could have kept in with the powers, toadied, joined the popular line. Or he could have become disobedient, or grown like his friend Simpson of the *Rambler* who was obedient to the spiritual power of the Church but always flinging out aggressively, "flicking his whip at Bishops, cutting them in tender places, throwing stones at Sacred Congregations, and, as he rides along the high road, discharging peashooters at Cardinals who happen by bad luck to look out of the window".

Newman was none of these things. He continued, snubbed as he was, in his own wide wisdom. Intelligence, courage, vitality, real thought must go with obedience, patience, humility. Of course life was difficult for him because he was a prophet and before his time. So many of the things he advocated are taken for granted now: peaceful dealing with those outside the Catholic Church, for instance, and encouragement to lay people to bear their part in the work of the Church.

Monsignor Talbot, in one of his most extraordinary

utterances, said that it was the province of the laity "to hunt, to shoot, to entertain" and in other matters they had better keep out. He would not get away with that statement to-day. In fact, when we see what exactly Newman was being blamed for, a hundred years ago, it is hard to see what all the fuss was about.

At the deepest level, he knew himself that all would be well. God had observed, God would deal with it all. Shut up the Job book. The words of Job were ended.

One morning Newman woke up very early, stuck his nose outside the covers and felt more discouraged than usual. In a few minutes it would be time to get up, and he usually took a cold showerbath. He had discovered, on a rare visit to the seaside, that bathing done in the ponderous Victorian fashion from a "machine" did him good, and when he got home he determined to continue his cold dips. Also he had his room papered, had double windows put in and matting on the floor. He did all this in a big effort to stop the heavy colds that came on him like blizzards. He had tried little remedies like sucking liquorice and using pepper, but his colds needed more combating than that.

Now to-day he could not bring himself to go along to his showerbath. Newman, who, when he was seventeen, always got up before the servants at Trinity and lit his own fire in the damp cold of an Oxford winter, was not the man to quibble at early rising and cold water. But he took his bath for his health, and really he wondered what was the use. Why bother? He did not see why he should go on cumbering the ground, and he muttered to himself, "What is the good of trying to preserve or increase strength, when nothing comes of it?"

Then he got up. He did not take his shower, but he was down in the sacristy vested for Mass, punctual to the minute. He said Mass, quietly, with no mannerisms, but making his own "speaking pauses" when he said the Pater Noster. At Mass he united his sufferings with Christ on the cross, and he found strength again for another day. At the end of Mass, he blew out the candles himself, took off his vestments, settled in a quiet corner of the church for more prayer. He had his own recipe for becoming a saint: it was to do perfectly all that was to be done in the day. No more and no less. His day might mean beginning some large work for God, it might mean having to take yet another snub, it might mean doing the routine work of a Birmingham parish. Just a day for God, and to-morrow there would be another one. There would also be Mass again, and fresh grace.

He rose from his knees and went along to the Oratory house. If you saw his face in repose it was gaunt and sad, with deep lines scored by sorrows. But it could lighten easily and from the sweetness of his manner you would never guess that anything was ever wrong.

Later in the day he would be found in church again, holding his hands behind his head, very still in front of the Blessed Sacrament. He prayed:

It has been my lifelong prayer, and Thou hast granted it, that I should be set aside in this world. Now then let me make it once again. O Lord, bless what I write, and prosper it—let it do much good, let it have much success; but let no praise come to me in my lifetime . . .

Let me learn more and more from Thy grace to be despised, and to despise being despised.

O Lord, help me—and Philip help me.

And again, O teach me how to employ myself most profitably, most to Thy glory, in such years as remain to me, for my apparent ill success discourages me much.

19 — A Cold but Bright Wintertime

Just once, in all those long years, did Newman have the chance of a straight fight, in public. It was a strange battle and Newman started off handicapped, but he won a most resounding victory.

In 1863 an astonishing statement appeared in a magazine. It was this:

> Truth for its own sake has never been a virtue with the Roman clergy. Father Newman informs us that it need not, and, on the whole, ought not to be.

The initials of the writer were C.K.; they were those of Charles Kingsley, who wrote *The Water Babies* and *Westward Ho*. Newman protested and Kingsley "apologised", saying that he had mistaken Newman's meaning.

"*Mean* it! I maintain I never *said* it!" said Newman, more nettled by the explanation than by the original insult. Now, since Kingsley had attacked all Catholic priests by his words, Newman had to clear up this matter; he could not leave people in any doubt about whether truth mattered to the Roman clergy, or whether he had said that lying was permissible and good. He joined battle in print and Kingsley retaliated with some more elaborate jeers. It was going to be difficult for Newman to clear his name. If he presented his case well, Kingsley would say to the public that here was one more example of Father Newman's craft and slippery skill with words.

What could be done to prove to all that he was no supporter of lies? It was not enough to fight on the narrow ground of whether or not he had ever said the things Kingsley claimed he had; he must do battle over a much wider area. Perhaps Kingsley had voiced, boldly and rudely, an idea that was in many minds—that Newman was a crafty man and that his conversion had been in some way dishonest.

"I must give the true key to my whole life", he said. What would that entail? He knew what he must do, and he would do it, though he shrank from the greatness of the task and from having to show his thought to the world. "I will draw out, as far as may be, the history of my mind."

So he began to write the story of his religious opinions, showing how they had developed over the years. He would trace the history of the Oxford Movement, of his own part in it, and people should see him as he really was. The work was to come out as a serial, and he must write hard and fast, or the public's attention would go. He wrote for two months, almost without resting, working sixteen hours, and more, in a day. To be exact in his account, he wrote to his old Anglican friends, such as Richard Church who had been one of the Proctors who had stood by Newman on that snowy day all those years before, when he had been proposed for condemnation by the University. Church and other old friends could check the facts, and they were very willing to help.

To recreate those distant scenes was a labour, a strain and a grief. Sometimes Newman bowed his head over his writing and wept—not easy, sentimental tears for earlier times, but hot, bitter, painful drops. One of the Oratorians would go in sometimes to that shabby, cluttered room. There was no sound but the scratching of a pen and the slight rustle of papers.

"The printer's man is here, Father."

The Father gathered the little sheaf, just ready in time, and smiled his courteous smile. The priest noticed his worn look and he felt concerned. As he went out, he saw Newman rub his stiff hands and wrists, and then turn to his work again. The printer's man carried away the sheets,

He had part of a little masterpiece there, written with such clear precision and such evident sincerity that all

England was captured by it. The book was called *Apologia Pro Vita Sua*, an explanation of his own life. The history of a man's religious opinions does not sound a popular subject, but each instalment sold like a batch of delicious cakes as it came hot from the press.

No one called him dishonest now. His old Anglican friends rejoiced at his success; the Catholics rallied round him again, especially Ullathorne and some of the "old" Catholics. Newman himself felt like a man who had been thrown into the sea. He had swum ashore, against heavy, cold waves and treacherous currents, and at last, the *Apologia* finished, he had reached the shore and lay there, a spent swimmer.

Kingsley had nothing to say except that Newman was like a treacherous ape who first looks with meek eyes "till he has you within his reach, and then springs gibbering and biting at your face".

Newman became popular all at once (except with Kingsley). His postbag became fatter than ever, and the letters now came in from overseas too. Some American babies, born in 1864, were christened Newman, and Newman K. Jones and Newman Aloysius Flanagan and such carried to the end of their days the proclamation that they were born in the year of the *Apologia* and that their parents were captured by the enthusiasm of the day.

So Newman was not a back number. He was powerful still. If his opinions were wrong-headed, as Manning thought, he was indeed a most dangerous man. He was treated like one, and as far as the most powerful men in the Church went, Manning and the authorities in Rome, he had to live in the cold shade of their displeasure.

So the sixties and the seventies passed, and Newman grew to be like a plant that is used to a chilly climate. He felt that if things were changed he would not know how to live in gentle warmth. His wintertime was not frozen or sad. The sharp winds blew on him, but he became less and less discouraged as time went on. He spent a brisk old age, working, walking, writing hard. He seemed to generate his own light and warmth, and his winter years had in them a hint of spring, putting out little shoots of vigour and hope.

His friendships multiplied and, especially after the publication of the *Apologia*, some of his old Anglican friends came back into his life. Richard Church, who had been delighted to help with the facts for the book, was even more delighted to see Newman again. Other old friends who came into view as well were not so comfortable in the renewal of friendship. In the summer of 1865 Newman went to visit Keble. Pusey was staying at Keble's house and, after twenty years, the three men who had once worked so closely together, met again. They sat round Keble's table and eyed one another narrowly. Newman thought how stout Pusey had grown and found his manner rather condescending. Pusey probably thought Newman should have grown stouter too: he found him gaunt and old. Keble, the middle man for size, contrived to be more easy in manner, more his old self. Newman felt a warmth and sympathy between himself and Keble still. They were all three kind and polite and all a little restrained. It was a charitable gathering and on the whole a sad one. They felt glad to see one another again—and how glad they were too when the day was over! Newman sighed with relief to be home again.

The work of the Oratory went on, of course, and, when he was free Newman spread his working papers on his big desk. He wrote letters and more letters and revised some of his books. By now he had a long bookshelf of works to his credit. There were historical books, volumes of sermons, essays, his novel, *Loss and Gain*, and another one about a martyr of the early Church called *Callista*. There was the little, important *Apologia*. There were his University discourses, his *Development of Doctrine* and a later book called *The Grammar of Assent* which went into a subject that had interested him for years, how a man comes to faith, and what can be the processes of his mind as he progresses towards it. His verses were bound in a volume too, and amongst them was a strange and moving poem, longer than his other verses, called *The Dream of Gerontius*.

It is the story of death and life after death. Gerontius dies, supported by his own trust in God and by the prayers of his friends on earth and in heaven. The devils are disappointed that he has escaped their clutches for he is to go to heaven, after a spell in purgatory. His guardian angel takes him there, and he learns how the Christian soul, when it sees the beauty and purity of God, longs for the cleansing suffering that will make it ready for life with Him. As the angel approaches the throne of God with Gerontius they hear the choirs of angels singing "Praise to the Holiest in the height". It is a song that has found its way out of the original story and into the hymn-books.

Later, the composer Edward Elgar set *The Dream of Gerontius* to music, to a fine operatic sort of score with plenty of contrasts. He has a wild music for the devils screeching "Ha! Ha!" and a very calm and lovely melody for the angel's song of triumph. When Elgar had finished, he wrote across his manuscript, "This was the best of me".

Gerontius was not Newman's best, but it had a strange power. He wrote as though he knew directly about purgatory, and his poem is unearthly but real. It grew from his own meditations on death and life after death; he was schooled to such meditations by the deaths of his friends and by his own frail health. The doctors often shook their heads and said that after so many years of overstrain Father Newman could not last long. But he confounded the doctors and his own fears to become, in his seventies, a dear old creaking door, stronger on its hinges than formerly.

Holidays were usually taken at a little house at Rednal, a village outside Birmingham, where Newman had acquired a country retreat for the Oratorians. Nowadays most people would go from the Hagley Road to Rednal by car or by two buses, and would not think of getting there on their own two feet—but more often than not Newman walked there, very rapidly, making his turns sharply. Eventually Ambrose St John bought one of the little carriages called a "basket" and they drove out there together. Newman complained, however, that it was hard to get Ambrose out except on Sunday, for he was a parish priest right through and usually took a walk in the parish area where he could work in a sick call or two. Out at Rednal Ambrose pottered about with the plants, and smoked a cigar if he had one. Newman avoided his fumes and urged him to look after his asthma. He had more sympathy with Ambrose's gardening activities and planted some trees in the garden himself.

There were always animals at Rednal, dogs and cats who belonged to the caretaker. One strong-minded dog was called Nero; he refused to eat biscuit and, said Newman, was "starving for lack of bones". Best loved of all was an old pony called Charlie who ended his days peacefully cropping the grass in a field at Rednal, making friends with an impudent young donkey who had joined him. When he died he was buried under two sycamore trees, and was remembered as a faithful friend—not, presumably, by the donkey, but by the Oratorians.

The fresh air of Rednal was a recreation for others too. The orphan boys went out there, and pulled the donkey's tail. The Oratory Schoolboys were out there often for feast-day picnics and celebrations. Groups from the parish went too. Once Father Ambrose took some of the rough Brummagem girls for a trip, and one of them fell down a hill. Her hat was askew, and it was difficult to hear what she said, since she had a thick, Midland voice, and had knocked two of her teeth out. "Ow, Father", she said, dirty but grinning, "it's the best day Oi've ever 'ad!"

Sometimes Newman was alone at Rednal, and then he played his fiddle to the cabbages and roses. He had an excellent instrument now, the first good fiddle he had had since he started playing at the age of ten. It was given him by his old friends Church and Rogers. A selection had come for him to choose from and he tried them so zealously that he had to have dabs of sticking plaster on his finger ends for days afterwards. When he was able, he took his chosen new fiddle and played his favourite Beethoven, who, he said, was like "a gigantic nightingale", "a great bird singing". He slept better and thought more clearly after he had been playing; music was his ease and his enrichment.

Later still, when his old fingers had become clumsy and he could only fumble with the strings, he sent his good instrument to Mary Church when her sister Helen got married. A violin was no substitute for a sister, but it would make up a little. When Helen and Mary were only children they made a great friend of Newman and sent him *Alice in Wonderland* and *The Hunting of the Snark*.

Many he had known as children were growing up. John and Charles Bowden, for instance, were mature priests at the London Oratory. His own nephews and nieces, Jemima's family and Harriett's one daughter, were grown up, and at last came to see him. He was very sad that Jemima waited until they were both old before she laid aside her angry feelings at his conversion.

Other children came to be Newman's friends; he had an endless supply all his life. They never forgot him, however long they lived. One little girl went to make her first confession to him at the Oratory and burst into tears through fright. She set up such a bawling that she did not hear the agitated rustling on the other side of the partition; Father Newman was busy climbing out of his side of the confessional so that he could come round to be comforting.

One little boy called Charles Marson lived near the Oratory, and looking from the passage window, he often saw "Mr John Henry Newman", as he thought of him, pass the house, clad in a loose coat and with a scarf tucked round the lower part of his face. His big nose stuck out over the scarf and he looked "sharp and saintly", Charles thought. Mr Marson was a very stern no-Popery Evangelical, and he spoke harshly of Mr Newman, a man who had gone astray and had led others astray too. Charles looked at him with pity and interest; he knew his father thought that Mr Newman would go to hell.

Now Charles kept guinea-pigs, and when he had enough pocket-money he went into the centre of Birmingham to the Market Hall to buy another one. As every Birmingham child knew, before the 1939 war, that was the place to go to buy small pets. Puppies, kittens, rabbits, guinea-pigs were all to be seen there, scrambling over each other in over-small cages. When the Market Hall was bombed during the war, the tiny animals escaped and ran about the streets.

One day Charles went in and bought a little guinea-pig; the man said he was called Sugarplum, and put him in a paper bag. Charles set off for the longish walk home, and he was perturbed to see big street louts on his route. He was not so much afraid for himself as for Sugarplum who was rustling in his bag. Every so often Charles peeped in to see that precious guinea-pig twitching his nose, or he put his hand in to feel his warm furriness. He was pleased to see a familiar, elderly figure in shabby black clothes coming from New Street Station and heading in the Edgbaston direction; Charles could walk close to him for protection. After a time Newman smiled and said, "What is your name, little fellow?"

"Please, Mr John Henry Newman, I am Charles Marson, and I am staying near you, and I have got two guinea-pigs and this little one which the man says is called Sugarplum."

Now Newman loved going to the Zoo to observe the animals and had been known to stand by a cage of beavers by the hour. Guinea-pigs were new to him, however, and he was the listener for the greater part of the dialogue they had along the way. This was not the last time they met. Charles would always bow low and Newman would laugh and enquire after Sugarplum. Once they went from the cross roads called Five Ways to the "Plough & Harrow" just by the Oratory, hand in hand, all the way. They did not talk that time but walked in a friendly silence. When they parted Newman patted Charles' head and said, "Be a good boy and love God".

Charles Marson never forgot the words, never forgot those small incidents. He knew that his Mr Newman was a very special person, at once very human and kind and also awe-inspiring and impressive. There was nothing more comfortable than to go down the Hagley Road with your hand in that warm and bony hand—and you could never be quite the same after he had said "Be good, and love God".

The children grew up, the older friends changed and died, falling like leaves from a tree. Newman's brothers grew old. Frank became odd but distinguished and wore a curious goat's beard that sprouted, hair by hair, from the middle of his chin. Charles continued to be odd, and lived obscurely. Their noses stuck out more in age, as did that of their venerable brother.

One old friend disappeared from view. That was Miss Maria Giberne, who, when she was nearly sixty years old, made up her mind to be a nun, and entered the convent of the Visitation at Autun. She was a lady of sturdy independence and might not have taken kindly to a life of obedience, but she stayed the course.

Old men expect to see the death of some of their contemporaries. It was Newman's great sorrow to see a younger man die, his greatest friend, Father Ambrose St John. He became very ill after sunstroke. For some time it was thought that he might lose his reason, but then he grew much better and the doctor thought he would make a good recovery. One day, when Newman sat by him, Ambrose held him closely round the neck, and then clasped his hand so tightly that it hurt. He could not talk clearly then, so that no one knew what to make of his actions. Newman knew afterwards that it was his "last sign of love". That night, at midnight, Newman was roused. Father Ambrose had taken a turn for the worse. When Newman reached him he found him already dead.

Newman mourned him deeply. He knew how much

Ambrose St John had been devoted to him; "as far as this world went", he said of his friend, "I was his first and last". He reproached himself that Father Ambrose overworked, and he wondered if he could have expressed to him more clearly his own gratitude and affection. People often feel, when their friends have gone from them, that they could have done more, said more. In fact, Newman need not have felt like this. At the end of the *Apologia* he had expressed in moving words how he felt gratitude for the goodness and friendship of all his Oratorians and especially of Ambrose St John, and he was as careful for them as they were for him.

At the funeral Newman broke down as he was giving the absolutions, and a noise, a ripple, went over the whole vast congregation. They were crying too.

Ambrose St John was buried out at Rednal, and Newman planted St-John's-wort there, round about his grave.

Success meant less than ever now. Newman did not expect that his peaceful, busy life would ever be disturbed again. He would go on much the same until he died and was buried out at Rednal himself. But there he was wrong. First a small but pleasant triumph came his way. Trinity College, his first college at Oxford, offered him an honorary Fellowship, and he was really pleased to accept the honour.

So at long last he went back to Oxford, saw his own old rooms again, and met Mr Short who was now very old indeed, and quite blind. "Dear Newman!" said the old Tutor, shuffling along to grasp his hand, and remembering the distant day when he had fed young Newman on lamb cutlets and sent him off to win the Oriel Fellowship.

It was strange to come back after so very long, to the place where he had intended to remain a scholar. He remembered the snapdragon which had grown outside his rooms, the flower he had taken as a sign of his perpetual residence in the University. An odd flower, his friends would say, for Newman's emblem, for it is a spiky plant with a bad tempered name. But if they saw the old flower-riddle verse, written lightly in a holiday time in 1827 in Mrs Rickards' album, they would think it is the right flower, though the original choice was made for a reason that did not hold.

It is a sturdy plant that can stand transplanting into miserable soil. It blooms cheerfully among stones. The "flowers of favour" said the Snapdragon in the verse, the rose, the lily, the dahlia, could bloom where they pleased.

> Pleasure, wealth, birth, knowledge, power,
> These have each an emblem flower;
> So for me alone remains
> Lowly thought and cheerful pains.

It is the flower of courage, and it should be Newman's plant still.

He would see the stones and flowers of Trinity once more in his life but, to his own great surprise, there was a bigger triumph first.

Upstairs at the Oratory Newman had a very curious, stiff piece of paper, originally the back cover of a school exercise book. He had made jottings on it over a long period of years, the first one written when he was eleven years old.

It ran like this:

John Newman wrote this just before he was going up to Greek on Tuesday, June 10th 1812, when it only wanted three days to his going home, thinking of the time (at home) when looking at this he shall recollect when he did it.

At school now back again.

And now at Alton, where he never expected to be, being lately come for the Vacation from Oxford where he dared not hope to be—how quick time passes and how ignorant are we of futurity. April 8th 1819. Thursday.

And now at Oxford but with far different feelings—let the date speak—Friday February 16th 1821.

And now in my rooms at Oriel College, a Tutor, a Parish Priest and Fellow, having suffered much, slowly advancing to what is good and holy, and led on by God's hand, blindly, not knowing whither he is taking me. Even so, O Lord. September 7, 1829. Monday morning ¼ past 10.

And now a Catholic at Maryvale and expecting soon to set out for Rome. May 29, 1846.

And now a Priest and Father of the Oratory having just received the degree of Doctor from the Holy Father. September 23, 1850.

The paper lay untouched for another thirty years, and then Newman wrote on the bottom:

And now a Cardinal.

Most of the entries were in pencil, but this one he did in ink. It deserved to be in letters of gold.

20 — The Lifting of the Cloud

When Newman had become an old man, in 1878, Pope Pius IX died and his successor was Pope Leo XIII, a forceful man who had many ideas in common with Newman. He received a request from the Duke of Norfolk and other influential lay people that he should make Newman a Cardinal and, since he had long admired him himself, he asked a certain Cardinal Nina to write to Manning to write to Ullathorne to find out from old Father Newman how he would feel about "accepting the sacred purple", for by such devious routes did information travel to and from the Vatican.

Ullathorne could not go over to the Oratory because he had a bad cold, so he wrote to Newman to go over to see him at Oscott. But Newman had to send another priest as his messenger, because he was in bed with a cold himself! Eventually Newman did discuss the matter with Ullathorne and then drafted a careful letter to Cardinal Nina. He was in a difficulty about what he should say for, on the one hand, he would be very glad to accept this honour from the Pope, which would show the world once and for all that Rome approved of him and thought him a whole-hearted Catholic and, on the other hand, he did not want to become a Cardinal if it meant that he must go to live in Rome. Cardinals (unless they are Archbishops too, Administrators in their own countries) usually have to go to Rome and Newman felt he was now too old and infirm to leave his home. Yet he did not like, plainly and rudely, to give the Pope conditions for offering the Cardinal's Hat. So his letter was delicately phrased.

Ullathorne saw that it might be interpreted as a refusal so, taking no chances (for he was greatly in favour of the Pope's suggestion) he wrote a covering letter to Cardinal Nina explaining further. Unfortunately all this correspondence must go through Manning's hands, so he put in another explanatory letter to Manning himself.

Manning took out Ullathorne's letters and sent Newman's letter by itself to Rome. The Pope would think that Newman did not want to be a Cardinal, and that, to Manning's mind, would be the end of an unfortunate incident.

Then there was a leakage of information and the English newspapers published a report that the Cardinal's Hat had been offered to Newman and he had refused it. Catholics were sorry to hear it and Protestants felt it was a good slap in the eye for the Pope. He could keep his Hats. *Punch* published a rhyme:

A Cardinal's Hat! Fancy Newman in that
For a crown o'er his grey temples spread :
'Tis the good and great head that would honour the Hat
Not the Hat that would honour the head.

There's many a priest craves it : no wonder *he* waives it
Or that we the soiled head-cover scanning
Exclaim with one breath, sans distinction of faith,
Would they wish Newman ranked with old Manning?

Newman sat at home in the Oratory, realising that some
unfortunate misunderstanding had taken place. How rude
it would seem to the Pope that Newman had refused the
honour before ever it had been offered him!

But the young Duke of Norfolk was determined to see
the matter through, and even more determined was the
dogged Ullathorne. He saw the hand of Manning somewhere in all this. He respected Manning's qualities but he
did not like his methods. It irked him to think that Manning took such a grand view of his own opinions. Once
Ullathorne was heard to growl (or so the story goes), "Manning? Why, I 'ad a mitre on my 'ead when 'e was still an
'eretic!" He had grown to love Newman, and he believed
him to be a singularly honest and sincere man.

Letters flew about. The Pope was left in no doubt of
Newman's real feelings and Manning sent out civil letters
to all parties saying how glad he was Newman had not
refused. He had quite misunderstood him the first time, he
said.

So at last the formal offer of a Cardinal's Hat came from
Rome, and Newman was glad to accept it. Now his obedience and loyalty were recognised. "The cloud has lifted,"
he said. "The cloud has lifted from me for ever."

He went to Rome with Father William Neville. Two
other Oratorians, already in Rome, would meet them
there. Father William was devoted to Newman and occasionally behaved rather like a Nanny entrusted with a
precious and delicate child. It was a good thing he was at
hand this time, for the weather turned cold (it was seldom

"sunny Italy" for Newman's visits) and the old man caught a chill.

Mercifully he was fit enough when they were first in Rome and he went to see the Pope. He came into the presence of a thin, shrewd looking man, with a clever skull and forehead. When Newman lifted his head after greeting the Pope he found himself looking into a pair of very bright, dark eyes. He saw that the Pope had a large, thin mouth with a quirk in it, and that he looked eager and affectionate. Meanwhile he had taken Newman's hand in his, and he kept it there throughout the interview. He asked after the members of the Oratory: how did they live, and who did the cooking for them? How many were they?

"We have lost some," said Newman, and his face clouded at the thought of Ambrose St John's death.

The Pope put his hand on his head in a comforting way and said, "Don't cry."

Then after a time, the other Oratorians came in too, and the Pope greeted them warmly. He told them—with Newman still there to hear it all—how much he admired him, and how glad he was to make him a Cardinal, and he said, to their further comfort, "I won't take him away from you. I leave him to be your father and superior and guide, and to be a blessing to England."

Then they left, but Pope Leo did not let Newman go from his presence without one more sign of his regard. He took his arm and escorted him to the outer door. The Oratorians fell in respectfully behind and looked with pleasure at those two venerable backs, the Pope in a white cassock and the Father in a black one. It was good to see that he was being treated with such honour. He was looking rather bowled over by it all himself, but they felt he was getting just what he deserved.

In his robes and amongst the other Cardinals they thought he looked splendid and the most venerable of them all. They did not think they were partial, either, for at the public consistory, when the Hats were given out, he seemed to attract a lot of attention. There was a babble and a whispering and the name "Newman" was repeated, set in phrases in different languages.

Gratifying as it was to be shown such honour and affection, these occasions meant more to Newman than this. He knew he had been placed in this position so that he could have a last opportunity to speak out for God. It was important that he should speak his best, for now he would be listened to.

He prepared and delivered a speech at a gathering just before the Consistory. His cold had been very bad, and he was tired and ill. Yet he managed to speak well, clearly and with feeling. There was a crowd of people, English and Americans who were in Rome, priests, Italian noblemen and ladies. They found themselves listening spellbound to his every word, nor could they take their eyes from his face. Newman's face was always interesting, and very different at different times. It could look very sad, or craggy, or rather grim, or extraordinarily bright when he smiled. Sometimes he looked ugly. To-day he looked pale and very beautiful. The English ladies said nothing but the Italian ladies rustled their silk crinolines and murmured, "Che bel vecchio! Che figura!" "What a beautiful old man."

He told them in his speech that all his life he had fought one enemy, and that was Liberalism. Now what did he mean by that? (For Liberalism is a word that has different meanings.) He meant the spirit that puts human things first, that teaches that religion is not true. More and more, he said, people would think less of God, and talk of religion as if it were just an opinion, a fancy, a kind of luxury. They would think they could get on very well without it. This was a terrible and a growing evil in the world—but even so, Christians need not fear, for all was in God's hands. Ultimately, he said, "the humble people will inherit the earth".

Newman could give his message in many ways, at length in a book, or in a speech, or even in a phrase. Now he had to see about his Cardinal's coat of arms and choose a motto for it. He chose with care and in four Latin words he gave men a summary of much that he had believed and practised all his life. In the Christian religion you do not just hold by a set of doctrines, but you love the person of Christ. God speaks to you, and you speak to Him. And in all human relationships the same truth holds—you cannot pass on ideas or advice or orders as though you were handing on a parcel. As a priest, a teacher, a friend, Newman had always tried to speak as a person to a person, directly, with insight and with love.

So now there was his motto, for all to see: *Cor ad cor loquitur.* "Heart speaks to heart."

When the ceremonies were over and Newman had done all he should, his fatigue overcame him, and he became really ill. So he could not visit in Rome, or go round the shrines, or do a great many things he would like to do. He could not even say Mass for most of his time there.

Now it was time to go, and there were presents to pack, and a whole trunkful of special clothes and vestments. The new Cardinal said it was a shocking waste, and he grumbled over the tailor's bill even though he did not have to pay it, for the Duke of Norfolk and other lay friends had kindly offered to pay all such expenses.

There was a last disappointment. Newman meant to visit Sister Maria Pia Giberne in her convent at Autun on the way home. She was most anxious to see him, and he would have great pleasure in seeing her. There was no other friend left now, with whom he could talk about old times, and recall his sister Mary who was still so dear to him. The doctor forbade him to make this extra effort, so the visit was not made. Newman sent Sister Maria Pia a letter which said, "We must submit ourselves to the Will of God. What is our religion if we can't?" No doubt she did try to be patient under her own disappointment, and no doubt it cost her very much. It was unlikely they would ever meet again, and indeed, they never did.

England at last, and one further ceremony. All England

had been interested and excited at Newman's honours, his Roman visit, his speech (which was relayed back by telegraph and printed in the newspapers), and now they welcomed him back most cordially. All Englishmen were glad, and especially the Catholics, and of the Catholics, especially the ones in Birmingham, and of the Catholics in Birmingham most especially the ones at the Oratory who could hardly wait for his return. A closed carriage was waiting for him at the station, and, as the horses trotted off in the direction of Hagley Road, a priest helped the Cardinal out of his black travelling clothes into his red-trimmed cassock, red skull cap and cloak, so that the waiting crowd at the Oratory should have all the fun of seeing him step out in full rig.

He came and the word was passed along. The congregation in the church got to their knees and the organ struck up.

After his entrance, and some prayers and ceremonies, the Cardinal's throne was moved into the centre of the sanctuary. Newman sat down, leaned his head on his hand, and looked at them all. He was happily conscious that his Oratorians were standing grouped round him in the sanctuary, and he sensed that this great crowd was genuinely delighted to see him back. There had been times in his illness abroad when he had wondered whether he would ever accomplish this return.

The crowd waited for his first words (his address would be something very stately, perhaps, as befitted a Cardinal) and while they waited, they had a really good look at him. Illness had made his face pale and transparent, almost unearthly. His ivory skin and his silver hair seemed to reflect rose tints from the bright, strong colour of his Cardinal's robes. He was lovely to see.

Then he said, rather softly, "It is such happiness to come home!"

"Newman returns from Rome a Cardinal"

21 — *Newman mounts an Eminence*

Newman came back to England into a blaze of glory, which was a strange and tiring experience for a delicate old man of nearly eighty who had lived humbly and obscurely for years. He had to attend many functions in his honour, receive addresses and congratulations, and show himself publicly as a Prince of the Church. On one occasion he was to appear in state at the London Oratory, and the Duke of Norfolk sent his carriage to take him there He did not think too much of the splendour himself, but Father William Neville was extremely pleased to put him into a carriage with the ducal arms on the panels, and to see him bowl away, tucked about with special rugs and with two men in livery mounted up behind. The fashionable crowds on that Sunday all noticed that carriage and stared to catch a glint of scarlet within, and see that famous profile.

On another occasion he had perforce to go to London again to have his portrait painted by the fashionable artist, Millais. The artist liked his subject and called the Cardinal "a dear old boy". He also made a laborious joke, for, as he waved towards the raised dais that had been placed in his studio, he murmured, "Will your Eminence mount that eminence?" Newman occupied his time picking Millais' brains for scraps of artistic information that he could send to Sister Maria Pia Giberne who was still wielding her paintbrush.

On yet another London occasion Cardinal Newman met Cardinal Manning—and Manning kissed him! It must have been like meeting a splendid tiger who has been out for your blood for years, and who is now ready to give you an affectionate lick as though he had become your dear domestic cat.

All these functions were something of a worry and fatigue, and occasionally Newman nearly lost his confidence. Once William Neville took him to the station and saw that he had become very tottery and kept dropping his gloves. William picked up his gloves, fussed a little, and gave him a good swig from a brandy flask. He saw that train go out with some misgivings, but he need not have worried. Newman returned home quite brisk and pleased with himself. "I did splendidly!" he said to his Oratorians. He always did splendidly at the public gatherings although he was old and frail and quite unused to this sort of life, for he had great dignity. Did he ever chuckle to himself when he saw the noblemen assembled to do him honour and the great ladies going on their knees to him in salons, to think that once he had been the notorious Newman who had been mixed up in that nasty Achilli trial, nearly a jailbird and a person that no one respectable would care to meet?

Other places besides the capital wanted to honour him, and he went again to Trinity, Oxford, to be fêted. It was especially pleasant to be received there, for Trinity had not waited until he had been made a Cardinal before renewing acquaintance with him. There was a great programme of festivities this time, despite an angry article from an Oxford newspaper which asked how Trinity dare give bed and board to a Roman Cardinal who would have them all burned as heretics if he could. Newman appeared in Oxford in all his glory, his brave red against the grey stones, making the pattern that the snapdragon had always made there. In his little poem he had suggested rather fancifully that the snapdragon's fragrance was given to it as a mark of heaven's favour. At the end of his life, in God's Providence, Newman was clad in red silk like a snapdragon flower, and his goodness, which had been secret before, was shed around, a fragrance.

At home in his Oratory he need not endure grander

and he lived simply there, as he had always done. He was still called "The Father" in his own household, and not "His Eminence". He still came to recreation like everyone else, and indeed recreation would have been dull without him; and he still ate his meals with the others, even though he was becoming rather toothless and could not eat everything served. He told Maria Giberne, who had also lost some molars, that he advised against swallowing down meat she could not chew. "You are not an ostrich," he said.

As a Cardinal, Newman now had a little private chapel upstairs in the house. It was dedicated to St Francis de Sales and there was a big picture of the saint, painted by Maria Giberne. There were also rows of little pictures, mainly photographs, of Newman's friends. He cherished them all in his affectionate memory and remembered them in his Mass. His room at the Oratory has been kept just as it was, the altar is still there, and St Francis and the personal picture gallery, the Victorian photographs fading, and their subjects sometimes wearing that fixed look that came inevitably when you had to "watch the birdie" for a long time in front of an early camera.

Newman had, too, a little book, an "Anniversary Book" with a stitched cover that Mrs Pusey had worked for him years and years ago. She had written the name of the poor Pusey baby in it and given it to her friend Mr Newman who had christened the child before it died. He had by now written in rows and rows of names of those dear to him who had died: Mrs Pusey herself, Lucy, Dr Pusey, Hurrell Froude, Keble, Harriett and Jemima now, as well as Mary, Charles, who had died at Tenby not so long ago, old and odd, and a determined atheist; Henry Wilberforce, who had once said he would rather Newman die than that he should become a Catholic, and yet who lived and died a good Catholic himself. Hawkins, Golightly—for Newman always prayed for his enemies—Ambrose St John, Maria Giberne; the name went in eventually. And there were scores more.

As the years went on, people thought he would not be

able to add to that loving and sad list in his book, for surely he could not last long now himself. He became bent and walked with a stick, "doubled up like a shrimp". His eyesight grew dim, and at last the muscles of his hand refused to work any more and he had to lay down his pen after all those books, all those thousands of letters. He could not see to read his Breviary now, so he said the Rosary instead, on large beads because his fumbling fingers could not manage small ones.

His old friend Ullathorne had retired now, and lived at Oscott. Years before, on an early visit to Oscott, Newman had found it a windy place, where prodigious gales blew down the guest room chimney. Ullathorne found it windy too, but he liked it because he could sit in his room and pretend he was on the high seas as in his cabin-boy days. In better weather he went forth, and occasionally he met Newman. One visit moved him very much. Newman, at parting, asked if he would do him a favour. This is how Ullathorne went on with the story :

"What is it?" I asked. He glided down on his knees, bent down his venerable head and said, "Give me your blessing." What could I do with him before me in such a posture? I could not refuse without giving him great embarrassment. So I laid my hand on his head and said : "My dear Lord Cardinal, notwithstanding all laws to the contrary, I pray God to bless you, and that his Holy Spirit may be full in your heart." As I walked to the door, refusing to put on his biretta as he went with me, he said, "I have been indoors all my life, whilst you have battled for the Church in the world." I felt annihilated in his presence. There is a Saint in that man.

Later they met again, at the Dominican convent in Stone. The nuns were delighted to have those two distinguished old men visiting them, and of course offered them tea in the parlour, and no doubt put out their best tablecloth and china. Newman was too shaky to manage without spilling, so Ullathorne kindly held his cup to his lips.

So Ullathorne was the steadier of the two, but he died before his old friend, just the same. On his death-bed he uttered one plain, short sentiment, a phrase that was very Christian and very typical of Ullathorne.

"The Devil's an ass!" he said.

And there was Newman still, eighty-nine, and as frail as a late autumn leaf. He had been ten years a Cardinal and he was still very sound in mind and spirit, as striking a personality as ever, bearing his growing infirmity and weakness gently and humbly but not sinking into a passive state.

He was still ready for his special work of fostering peace and charity between Christians. There was a dispute in the Cadbury chocolate factory in Birmingham, for the Quaker employers wanted their Catholic work-girls to attend the prayer meetings held at work. Cardinal Newman was appealed to, and he went straight there, on a cold and snowy day, and talked to the employers, explaining matters so well that everyone was satisfied.

He said his last Mass on Christmas Day. After that he did not dare attempt it, for his fingers were too fumbling to hold the chalice safely. But he went through the actions and prayers of the Mass every day, with great devotion. If ever his strength should return he would be ready to say Mass again. But that day never came.

In June, 1962, a very old priest died at the Birmingham Oratory. He was Father Denis Sheil, and he was ninety-six. In his latter years he could not get out much, but occasionally he could visit friends and he dearly liked to go out to tea. Over his tea (preferably a good one with what he, in his old-fashioned way, called plum-cake), he would sometimes give his reminiscences, and scenes of long ago would come vividly into his memory, far more clear to his mind than what happened in 1960 or 1961. He remembered the funeral of Father Ambrose St John, when he was a boy at the Oratory School. He remembered Newman's grief, and the grief of all the congregation, and he also remembered the black cotton gloves that he and all the other boys were wearing.

He would recall, too, the August of 1890, when he was a young Oratorian novice, the last person to receive the Oratorian habit from Cardinal Newman's hands. The weather was hot, and he, Denis Sheil, was tired, and he longed for a spell out in the country at Rednal. He went and asked permission to go from the Father, and of course he got it. He had his brief holiday at Rednal and came home at the week-end, restored by sunshine and full of spirits. But when he got inside the Oratory house he found all was very quiet and people were going about looking grave and preoccupied. The father had taken cold and he was very ill in bed. Denis Sheil almost wished he had not been off enjoying himself.

Upstairs Newman lay unconscious, his nose and chin jutting more than ever. He was wearing a silk handkerchief round his neck, at his own request. That handkerchief had been given to him years ago, in one of his bad times, by a poor person. It was a present given with sincere love, and Newman had treasured it. The Oratorian fathers came in to look at that still face, and poor Father William tidied up the bed a bit, and realised that he would not be able to do anything for the Father again.

Perhaps Newman lay there in a dreamless sleep, or perhaps his memory was still at work so that he saw again some of the many scenes of his life, shifting like the patterns of a kaleidoscope, down the long, hard, busy years, until he saw a tiny boy playing in a garden. That little boy was so gifted that his mind readily received impressions of all the new and lovely world about him, and yet he knew, even then, that God was more real and dear than anyone or anything else.

Death is a lonely experience, and Newman died without any further speech or recognition of his friends. But it was always true that "he was never less alone than when alone", and God was with him. He slipped away peacefully, silently, on Monday evening, August 11th, 1890.

He had a splendid funeral, of course, and all England did him honour. *The Times* did not fill its columns, as a rule, with praise of Roman Cardinals, but it did this time, and the Birmingham journalists wrote with pride of their distinguished citizen.

The roads were lined with people all the way to Rednal, where the Oratorian cemetery is. The men from the Oratory parish did their part, and there are people in Birmingham to-day who will tell you with great pride that their grandfathers helped to carry Newman's coffin, on their shoulders, for part of the journey to its resting place.

22 — *The End and the Beginning*

So Newman died, but that was very far from being the end of the story. In his lifetime there were many people who loved and admired him, and who thought he was one of the best and the wisest men of his day. There were also a great many (and unfortunately they included some important and influential men) who overlooked him, who mistrusted and doubted him. He had to suffer the greatest humiliation and frustration that a man with a great mind and spirit can suffer—the knowledge that he had important things to say and that few would listen to the message. But since his death his voice has been heard more and more.

His books are read, his ideas are studied. In England, in Europe and America, the name of John Henry Newman is known and respected more and more, and in far-off places too, where you would not expect a ready, natural interest in him and his ideas; there are Newman study circles now in Athens and in the middle of Africa. He would not have cared much for such wide travel in his lifetime, shy and home-loving as he was, and so intensely English in many ways, but he would rejoice to see how his message goes forth to an ever-widening circle. There are so many different kinds of people to be interested in what he has to say; the historians, the people concerned with universities and schools, the theologians and philosophers, the literary men, the ordinary people who are interested in these subjects too, in their measure, and who think that Newman may help them to understand more of this world and of the next.

Many of his ideas were suspect in his own day, but now they are seen to be sound and good, and of great importance. If Newman were to come and haunt us, he could nod his wise head and say, over and over again, "I told you so!" He would do no such thing, of course; it is not a very civil remark and, even as a ghost, Newman would always be gentlemanly.

It is not only by reading his books that men come to be influenced by Newman. The story of his life is in itself a lesson and an influence. In his lifetime he was a magnet for people, and still they feel the force of his strong, attractive personality. He is with us still. He is not just a dead-and-gone author of many books, a person to set the learned rustling away in libraries all over the world, not just an old ecclesiastic whose large, fine head, with its great nose and sensitive mouth, its sad eyes, looks at us from the portraits and the sculptures. He is very much alive still.

If you visit the places he once lived in, you sometimes have a most extraordinary sense that time might move backwards so that we could have a glimpse of him. Try going into St Mary's church in Oxford, on a darkening winter afternoon, and look at the high pulpit. You can almost hear the hiss of ancient gas-lighting, almost see that spare figure mounting up there to preach one of the famous sermons.

Or go down Oriel Lane in an evening, an evening after rain so that the paving stones are wet and gleaming, and little runnels of water are coming down from the gutters of the lovely college roofs. If you are lucky and the time is quiet so that the roar of the traffic does not assault your ears and fix you quite irrevocably to the mid-twentieth century, you will feel that you are back in the older Oxford. A slight young man comes hurrying by. He is wearing knee-breeches, silk stockings (a bit wrinkled) and low, soft, slipper-like shoes, rather unsuitable for the weather. He has just come across the High, from his lodgings to dine in his new college, Oriel, and he has to wear the correct dress for the function. He picks his way carefully among the puddles and he looks greatly preoccupied. He must not be late, nor must he bespatter his shoes and stockings. You almost expect to hear him mutter, like the White Rabbit, and if he did he would say, "O dear, Copleston will be annoyed!" He is a nice-looking young man with soft hair that has already become untidy (and that will earn him another black mark from the Provost). His spectacles glint a little, and with a last hop round a puddle he disappears into Oriel. There is a spatter of silver raindrops and, as you blink and look again, you are back again in this present day and a modern undergraduate is splashing through on a bicycle.

Littlemore is a great place for conjuring up vivid pictures of Newman because it has been so beautifully restored to what it was in the eighteen-forties. There are even bulbs in the garden, just as though Bowles has been along recently, after rifling his mother's flower-beds, and there are nice, old-fashioned rose bushes which look as if Ambrose St John has been planting.

You can go into Newman's small austere room, very cold with its bare walls and uncarpeted brick floor, and you reflect what a mercy it was that there was a fire burning in the grate on that wild wet night when Father Dominic arrived straight from his tedious journey. It is a peaceful room, a happy place, for all its austerity. Next door you can see the chapel, its walls hung about just as they used to be so that the place is like a little red-lined box.

Mass is said there sometimes now. The second Mass in the Littlemore Oratory was in fact offered by the Catholic Archbishop of Birmingham in 1960. Well, you would expect someone important to re-open that small and holy place where Father Dominic said the first Mass and gave Holy Communion to the new converts. Father Dominic Barberi may be a canonised saint one day, and so may Newman.

Was Newman then, as well as being a great writer, thinker, preacher, and an important and influential man of his time, also a saint? Perhaps he was. Perhaps we shall live to see the day when he is officially acclaimed as such. His was a long life and a very interesting one, so marvellously shaped and all of a piece. He liked to look back over it himself and think of God's mercies to him, to see how the "Kindly Light" had led him over so many rough places in his life's journey. It was a sad life, in so many ways, and yet it is not a depressing one to hear about. It is a record of strong faith and hope, and of a very great charity. It has the beauty of holiness.

If a person's reputation for holiness grows after his death, the Bishop or Archbishop of the diocese where he lived may set up an official enquiry into his life and his writings. This is called "introducing a person's cause". All the evidence must be carefully sifted and, if it does indeed seem that this person's life was of unusual holiness, further investigations will be made from Rome. A further piece of evidence that will be required will be miracles, such as the curing of sick people in such a way that natural causes can be ruled out. It would, of course, be a clear sign of God's will in the matter to have miracles done when this person's aid is invoked, but it is the sure evidence of great holiness that is the important thing. Then the Pope may ultimately proclaim that man or woman "Blessed". Such a person is quite certainly in heaven and he is to be honoured and imitated by Christians here on earth. After the beatification, the person may be given greater honour still and be canonised by the Pope. Sometimes the time between beatification and canonisation is short and sometimes it is very long. You really cannot tell how it will be.

In 1958 the Archbishop of Birmingham introduced Newman's cause. And so now the investigation is afoot. His writings will have to be sifted, of course, and that is going to be a very long job. Since Newman was writing busily from the time he was a small boy at school to his extreme old age, when failing sight would have stopped anyone less conscientious and determined, and since he lived to be eighty-nine, the assessing of all his books, letters and diaries is a formidable task. So it is unlikely that there will be a quick decision.

One thing is certain. The introduction of his cause will itself create fresh interest. It is like a great stone thrown into the pool; the ripples widen and spread, and Newman's influence goes out farther than ever.

It is a strange fact about Newman that he influences this world so widely and so profoundly, and yet he did not really care for this world at all. He had his deep loves, his friends, the places he knew, books and learning, the beauties of this natural world, but his heart was not set on any of these things. He cared very much, and at the same time he did not care at all. He appreciated, so deeply and so delicately, all the good things here, but they all seemed to him a shadow and a dream, compared with God.

You feel this most, perhaps, when you stand by his grave. It is at Rednal, Birmingham. It is an outlying suburb now (it was a village in Newman's day) at the foot of the Lickey Hills. These hills are a great source of pride and pleasure to the Birmingham dwellers, and they go out there in droves at week-ends, and still more at Bank Holiday times to climb the slopes and to pick great bunches of bluebells, illegally, in the Spring. So there is a small shanty town there, stalls for selling candyfloss and hot dogs, and rather nasty ice-cream. The children swarm and the teddy-boys lounge there, idling at the pin-tables in the amusement arcade or playing the juke-boxes in the coffee bars. To find the Oratorians' country house you move down a quieter road and turn off by a winding path. In a minute or two you leave the noise and the shoddy little pleasure places and you are more conscious of the fresh and woody smells that come from the Lickeys just above you. Through a tangled shrubbery, and you are on to the lawns that front the Victorian house. The cemetery is reached simply by stepping from the garden itself. It is really just an extension, a little garden reached from the bigger one.

So the story began in a garden and ends in one (if "end" is the right word, since the end of Newman's life marks a great beginning). It is a very peaceful spot, with rows of humble graves, all marked with a simple cross. Each one tells you the name of the man who lies there, though not much else, for Oratorians do not have texts and tributes on their graves, and, as you read them, you recognise them, one after the other. At the end of the *Apologia* Newman spoke his gratitude to all his friends and brethren at the Oratory. You can almost hear that silver voice reading the list as you go from grave to grave :

I have closed this history of myself with St Philip's name upon St Philip's feast-day; and having done so, to whom can I more suitably offer it, as a memorial of affection and gratitude, than to St Philip's sons, my dearest brothers of this house, the Priests of the Birmingham Oratory . . . HENRY AUSTIN MILLS . . . EDWARD CASWALL . . . WILLIAM PAINE NEVILLE . . . and HENRY IGNATIUS DUDLEY RYDER—who have been so faithful to me; who have been so sensitive to my needs; who have been so indulgent to my failings; who have carried me through so many trials; who have grudged no sacrifice, if I asked for it; who have been so cheerful under discouragements of my causing; who have done so many good works, and let me have the credit of them; with whom I have lived so long, with whom I hope to die . . .

And then he paid his greatest tribute :

And to you especially, dear Ambrose St John, whom God gave me when he took everyone else away; who are the link between my old life and my new; who have now for twenty-one years been so devoted to me, so patient, so zealous, so tender; who have let me lean so hard upon you; who have watched me so narrowly; who have never thought of yourself if I was in question . . .

Here at last is the name of Ambrose St John on a grave and here is Newman's too. They are buried together because Newman wished it so. So here he lies, in the same grave with his great friend.

It is so very quiet here. This grave speaks, as all graves do, of the shortness of man's life, of the way this world so quickly passes for us. It speaks more convincingly than usual, but quietly and gently. It speaks as with Newman's voice. He was very conscious himself that death meant a passing to a much greater reality.

You can read his last word to us in the epitaph he wrote for himself. It is not on his grave but on a memorial stone at the Birmingham Oratory. The great church there is reached by going from the street through a sort of cloister. On one side it is open to a little Italianate court; on the other side there is a wall that commemorates all the dead Oratorians of that house by these memorial tablets set on it. One is larger than the others, and has the Cardinal's coat-of-arms carved above it. And there are Newman's famous words, his last message to us, a message to inspire us to think more seriously of Heaven: "He has passed from the realm of the shadows and the images, into the truth."

EX UMBRIS ET IMAGINIBUS IN VERITATEM